# Songs of the Spirit

Megan Daffern is Chaplain at Jesus College, Oxford, and a lecturer in the Faculty of Theology and Religion, University of Oxford. An Anglican priest and a member of the Third Order of the Society of St Francis, she combines pastoral and academic work in her ministry, and is passionate about communicating the Bible to a wide audience. She is married to Adrian, a rector and assistant archdeacon in the diocese of Oxford.

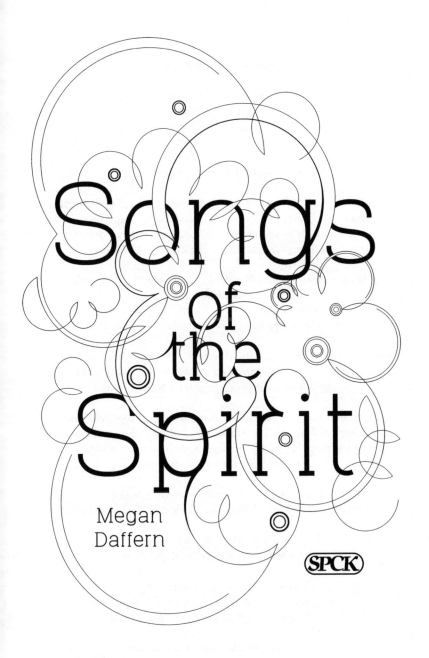

# Songs
## of
## the
## Spirit

Megan
Daffern

**SPCK**

A psalm a day for Lent and Easter

First published in Great Britain in 2017

Society for Promoting Christian Knowledge
36 Causton Street
London SW1P 4ST
www.spck.org.uk

The Scripture quotations are the author's own translation.

On p. 194, the verses of the metrical version of the 'Canticle of the Creatures'
are taken from *The Daily Office SSF*, published by the Society of St Francis
2010, with thanks to the brothers at Hilfield Friary.

*British Library Cataloguing-in-Publication Data*
A catalogue record for this book is available from the British Library

ISBN 978–0–281–07796–0
eBook ISBN 978–0–281–07797–7

Typeset by Manila Typesetting Company
First printed in Great Britain by Ashford Colour Press
Subsequently digitally printed in Great Britain

eBook by Manila Typesetting Company

Produced on paper from sustainable forests

# Contents

## Contents

## Contents

### *Week 7: Easter*
### A redeemed world

# Acknowledgements

Of all the brothers and sisters I would like to thank, I must pick out the following in particular:

Jesus College, Oxford, who have nurtured my voice as an academic and as a priest.

The Society of St Francis, particularly the Hilfield Community, who are all shepherds in one way or another.

My one-time supervisor and constant friend, John Barton, who models with humility how to be both an academic and a priest.

Philip Law, John Pritchard and the wider team at SPCK, who helped these spoken words to become written words.

And my husband, Adrian. He is an inspiration: he helps me to breathe – and sing.

SDG

# *Foreword*

I've loved the Psalms most of my life, but I've never been sure how to handle them. I sang them as a choirboy – Psalm 23 at a funeral, Psalm 67 at a wedding, Psalm 150 when we wanted to put on a show. I've used them for meditation, usually cherry-picking my favourites – 8, 16, 19, 27, 42, 63, 139 and so on. At Canterbury Cathedral I used to approach Evensong on the fifteenth day of the month with trepidation because it meant all 73 verses of Psalm 78 would have to be sung. The Psalms have been my companions throughout my Christian life.

But I've never been entirely relaxed with them, and I suspect I'm not alone. We know the Psalms are central to both Jewish and Christian devotion, but sometimes we find ourselves in strange territory, out of our depth or lurching from exquisite beauty to vitriolic anger. The Psalms can feel like an assortment of chocolates where you're never sure if the one you've chosen will be rich and sweet or bitter and harsh.

What we need is a wise interpreter, and here we have her. Megan Daffern has written an immensely valuable book which will help all of us fortunate enough to encounter it to relish the Psalms as a unique treasury of spiritual insights.

What Megan offers us is a rare integration of gifts. She clearly writes out of real scholarly understanding, but equally she writes with an immediacy and accessibility which will open the Psalms to anyone. Her translation is remarkably fresh and appealing, and opens up familiar lines in delightfully unexpected ways. Her way of handling the text is both intellectually illuminating and spiritually rich, washing mind and heart with understanding and love. And the innocent-looking questions at the end of each section are spot-on.

## Foreword

I couldn't look for more from a Lent book, particularly one I can re-read at any time of year.

This box of chocolates may be dangerous but it's also wonderfully tasty and deeply nourishing. I shall return often, asking for more.

*Bishop John Pritchard*

# A note on translation

---·•·---

The primary aim of this translation is to connect with its readers. Informed by a range of English translations as well as the LXX and Vulgate, I want the Hebrew text to resonate with our lived experience, in language suitable for as wide an audience as possible. This intention comes before the poetic style (which I raise from time to time in the reflections). Frequent exclamation marks draw attention to tone and speech-acts through syntax. Sometimes, instead of the well-rehearsed turns of phrase used in translations in church, I have made something strikingly different yet as true to the Hebrew as possible, in order that readers should not skip over words that seem familiar, but rather find themselves challenged to read the texts afresh. In all instances I would be pleased to share the explanation of my renditions. Should this little book contribute to academic debate regarding the Psalms or the Hebrew language, or prompt even the well-versed student of the Psalms to see something new in this wonderful text, then I delight in offering something not only to my primary audience, but also to those few scholars who may wish to engage with the Psalter through writing such as this as well as through learned journals.

As for idiom, because Hebrew prefers the masculine, 'he who does . . .' etc., I use male pronouns while understanding that these sayings apply to *everyone*, of whatever gender.

Verse numbers follow those given in the Hebrew version. The *Biblia Hebraica Stuttgartensia* follows the Leningrad Codex.

# Introduction

## Learning our place

———•◦•———

### In the bookshop . . . Choosing this book: mapping your Lent

Where are you? Are you a long-standing disciple of Jesus, or are you just wondering about giving it all a go? Are you unsure about how to keep Lent holy, or are you an old hand? Are you in a good place and looking for growth, or are you in a tough one and looking for some peace? Are you good at prayer, or do you find it hard to work out where to start?

If any of the above describe your situation, this book is written for you: whether you're a complete novice at doing Lent, or someone whose regular spiritual discipline often includes reading. It is an invitation to think about Lent through some of the oldest prayer traditions we have – the Psalms. It welcomes you to travel through Lent alongside Jesus, because this was his prayer book, too. Although the Psalms started life *before* Jesus, they are full of themes and experiences which fitted with his life and story, and which fit with our own lives and faith too.

There may be some familiar, comfortable psalms, and there will probably be some unfamiliar, challenging ones as well. These are Songs of the Spirit: the Holy Spirit can comfort the disturbed, and disturb the comfortable. But the life of faith gives us strength to face both joy and difficulty. The disciple dares to take on questions and challenges safe in the knowledge that alongside Jesus, our friend in prayer, we are guided towards true companionship, breaking bread with him and with one another.

We may think we control how we pray, that we're responsible for our own prayers. We decide what we pray, when we pray, what we say or think. But that's not the whole story. Prayer has a deeper value: it's about opening ourselves to God. About letting God in, and letting God be in charge. And how better to do that than through prayers used by generations of the faithful, prayers which Jesus himself joined in? By letting others' words shape our own prayers, we come closer to letting God himself shape how we pray.

These are prayers used for ages past and which will be used for ages to come. We are taking our place in a stream of prayer. These songs are timeless, making connections between past and present, between what mattered then and what matters now. Prayer looks forward: it is a hoping, an opening, a beginning. It is a starting point which helps us set our face to the kingdom of God. Looking upon God through the prayers of many generations, we open ourselves up to his gaze as much as we gaze upon him.

Whether you know it or not, that may be why you are choosing to spend this Lent with the Psalms: they are part of Jesus' journey, and part of your journey. My prayer for you this Lent is that wherever you are coming from and wherever you are going, you too can know peace whatever you face, saying with the Psalmist, and with Jesus:

I have smoothed down and quietened my soul,
just like a weaned child on his mother,
like a weaned child on my breast is my soul.

*(Psalm 131.2)*

## On Shrove Tuesday . . . Using this book: unfolding your Lent

Why have you chosen a Lent book as your way of keeping Lent? I hope you know that Lent isn't necessarily about giving something up (Chocolate? Gin and tonic? Puddings? Coffee? Facebook?) just to make yourself feel miserable. That wouldn't get us anywhere on our journey with Jesus – at worst it would make us grumpy and hinder us in how we *are* trying to serve God, while at best we may lose a few kilos and realize that not being obsessed with social media may actually be good for us. But what does it do for our relationship with Jesus? Probably not very much.

Perhaps that's why you've decided to do some reading and praying during Lent: to try and focus on Jesus and your spiritual life first and foremost, by yourself, or with others; to adopt a discipline that re-roots your faith in God.

Each day of Lent (not including Sundays, because Sundays are *always* days of celebration when Christians remember Jesus' death and resurrection) we will take a psalm, read it slowly, and reflect on it. We will make these aged prayers of Jesus' day our own prayers in our own day, in our own situations. Sometimes the reflections will make us ask questions, sometimes they will make us think. Praying, reading, questioning and thinking are all part of our spiritual journey and our growth in faith.

Groups can use the book too: very simply, each member in turn reads the day's psalm, then one person in the group (it can change week by week) leads conversation on what the week's psalms and questions have meant to us, and how we can pray them today.

It can be hard to carve out time each day to settle down and read slowly and reflectively. While it's best if you can read each section on the day it's meant to be read, don't worry if you fall behind; it's OK to read several in one sitting if that's what works for you. I admit that's how I often read a Lent book. Of course, if you are reading with a group, then you have committed to the others to be up to date with your reading when the group meets.

Sometimes spiritual disciplines can be a good way of holding ourselves to things. If I've solemnly decided to go on retreat three times a year, then I have even more reason to go. If I've devoted myself to a rule of life that says I should pray or read something each day, then it helps me to do just that. A plan for a spiritual journey is helpful for keeping us on track: a realistic promise holds us to a rhythm or habit that is good for us in our relationship with God. It's no coincidence that friars, sisters, monks and nuns wear 'habits'.

So you've chosen a Lent book, you've made a decision that you want to read and grow in your discipleship. Holding to a framework of discipleship, and letting yourself be steadied by that discipline, is about being a pupil, a student; about learning. Ash Wednesday then starts right there: with being a pupil in prayer.

# WHERE TO BEGIN?

# Ash Wednesday

## ABC: learning prayers

———◆•◆•◆———

## Psalm 25

1   Of David. To you, O Lord, I lift up my soul,

2   my God, in you I trust. May I have no cause for shame, may
my enemies not be glad to my cost.

3   May even anyone who waits faithfully for you have no reason
to be ashamed. Rather, let *them* be ashamed, those empty
souls who act faithlessly!

4   Your ways, O Lord: make me know them. Your paths: teach
them to me.

5   Make me tread the journey in your truth, and teach me;
because you, my God, are the God who saves me, I wait for
you every day.

6   Remember your compassion, O God, and your loving-kindness,
because from of old they have always been the same.

7   The sins of my early life and my rebellious years – may you not
remember those;
according to your loving-kindness, remember *me*, for the sake
of your goodness, O Lord!

8   Good, and right, is the Lord, and so he directs wrong-doers on
the journey.

9   He guides the poor along the path of justice, he teaches the
poor his path.

10   All the footpaths of the Lord are loving-kindness and truth, for
those who guard his pledged relationship and solemn charges.

11   For the sake of your name, O Lord, forgive all I am guilty of,
because it is immense.

12  Who is the man who fears the Lord? He will be the one to
    direct them on the journey they should choose.
13  Their souls will stay in goodness, and their children will inherit
    the land.
14  Intimacy with the Lord is for those who stand in awe of him,
    and his pledged relationship is to be made known to them.
15  I always look towards the Lord, because he leads my footsteps
    from getting tangled up.
16  Look at me, and be kind to me, because solitary, and poor, am I.
17  Widen the constrictions of my heart and help me out of tight
    corners.
18  Open your eyes to my poverty and my hard work, and lift my
    sins from me.
19  Look at my enemies, how many they are, with what hateful
    violence they hate me.
20  Keep my soul safe, and get me out of this, so that I may have
    no reason for shame because I have retreated to you.
21  May integrity and uprightness guard me, because I wait for
    you faithfully.
22  O God, pay the ransom for Israel from all that constrains it.

Like Psalm 25, many psalms have headings, often referring to David.
As we sing or hear psalms in church, we don't usually see their headings. David himself probably didn't write all the Psalms 'of David', or 'for
David': some, composed later, took his name in their titles because he
was the most famous psalm singer. With his music, he soothed Saul, the
very first king of Israel (1 Samuel 16). To his first wife's embarrassment
(2 Samuel 6), David sang and danced before the Ark of the Lord – the
sacred wooden portable cabinet which housed the tablets of the Law
which Moses had received from God. Because the memory of David
and his worship songs was so treasured, many psalms refer to David.

David's kingship over Israel was a golden age. Jesus was born in
Bethlehem, 'David's town', because David was the ancestor of Jesus'
earthly father Joseph. Jesus was regarded as the new David, the true
King, and was called 'Son of David': the very best Jewish ancestry. He
was joining David's house as a king, and he was joining in his ancestor's tradition as a psalm-singer.

But there's discontinuity between David and Jesus too. Jesus was without sin; David not so. David's relationship with Bathsheba involved killing her husband so he could take her as another wife (2 Samuel 11). Nathan the prophet told David how wrongly he had behaved. Psalm 51, the text of the searingly beautiful music of the 'Miserere' by Allegri often sung on Ash Wednesday, is claimed to depict David's penitence. David knows how to rejoice and be glad with psalms; he also knows how to repent and confess his sins.

Ash symbolizes repentance and death. Death because one day we'll no longer need our bodies: some of us will be cremated. 'Dust to dust, ashes to ashes . . .' go the words of the funeral service. Repentance because in the Old Testament one way of showing how sorry you were was to sit in a pile of rubbish and cover yourself with dust and ashes (Job 2).

Remembering our limits, sitting in dust and ashes: both are signs of humility. Lent is about humility. With humility we realize we aren't really so big after all, we don't know it all. This can be good news. We don't have to be the best, the most successful. If we are small, there is more room for others to be bigger, better than us. If we are humble, there is more room in our lives for God to be God. Humility is liberating.

Psalm 25 resounds with humility. Prayer itself is humble: we're saying we can't do it by ourselves. Asking for help can often be the biggest step for someone who's struggling. We don't want to be seen as needy, we want to look strong; yet the moment we acknowledge we're stuck is the moment we're freed to receive help. In Psalm 25 we keep asking for help. We're relying on someone other than ourselves. We're 'waiting faithfully': we know we need God.

Verses 6–7 call upon God's eternal love. Paradoxically, the Psalmist reminds God about his youthful errors, then asks God to forget them. What's still more important is that God remembers 'me', says the Psalmist. This confusion in an apparently 'textbook' prayer shows we too can be all over the place when we pray. We can rely on God to know what's best, to remember or to forget things *for our sakes*. The unchanging God beyond time and place transcends the frail and fragile changes within us. Aware of our wobbliness and God's steadiness, calling upon God helps us be more stably rooted.

The 'poor' in Psalm 25 are the humble, stricken or oppressed. It's about being downtrodden, small. We can think we are big, capable, good people, that we have what we need to look after ourselves. But if we live from the perspective of the poor, the small, the person on the margins, we more readily yearn to be guided, loved, looked after, taught (verses 9, 16, 18).

How we relate to God is about humility. God in Psalm 25 is nearly always called 'LORD'. This is the name YHWH, or 'Yahweh', which our Jewish brothers and sisters, in deep reverence for the proper name of God, pronounce 'Adonai', the Hebrew word 'Lord'. 'LORD' refers to the name of God revealed to Moses at the burning bush: YHWH, 'I AM WHO I AM' or 'I WILL BE WHO I WILL BE', the very holiest name there is. So when we say or read 'LORD' we do so in solidarity with everyone who calls upon God as 'LORD'. Together we are thinking both of the kingly God, great alongside our smallness, and the God who time and again bears with our mistakes and saves us. Our human story repeats itself, showing we can't keep up with God, or keep his covenant, the relationship he promises with his people. This is the 'pledged relationship' of verses 10 and 14. We are taking our tiny place among all those God wants to be in relationship with. Once again we think of how great God is, how little we are.

We learn most when we are little. When I play with my two-year-old niece, I often wonder what she's learning today. Perhaps the greatest thing we learn in our lives is *how to learn*. Do you still want to learn? Sermons may not always be memorable, but one that stays with me declared: 'To learn requires humility; to teach requires patience.' We were in a university setting, surrounded by teaching and learning. Learning is about humility. It is glorious to learn.

Poems, rhythmic sayings, help us remember things, such as the number of days in a month. Hymns and songs in church help us remember our faith, like 'The Lord's my shepherd, I'll not want.' A good Jew, like Jesus, would learn the Psalms by heart. Psalms are about learning – learning to pray, learning about God, practising our relationship with God. What better way to spend Lent than by learning about these prayers, and what they teach us about God?

*What do you most want to learn this Lent?*

# Thursday

## *Lifelong learning: from young . . .*

---

### Psalm 119.1–16

1   Blessed are they who have a secure footpath in life, walking in the instruction of the Lord.

2   Blessed are they who uphold the witnessed testimonies of the Lord, those who go back to him time and again in their hearts.

3   They do not commit even a single injustice, rather they walk in the footsteps of the Lord.

4   You have required your precepts to be kept with all diligence.

5   Oh, how I wish that every step I take could be firm in keeping your solemnly written word of instruction!

6   Then, I would not ever have the shame of getting anything wrong, because I would be paying attention to all your commandments.

7   May I praise you with a right heart, as I learn how you judge true righteousness.

8   I will keep your solemn instructions: may you never leave me!

9   How can a young man clean up his path in life? By keeping watch over it all according to your word.

10   With all my heart I have sought you; do not lead me away from your commandments.

11   Deep in my heart I treasure up your spoken word, so that I may not wrong you.

12   Blessed are you, O Lord; make me learn my obligations to you.

13   With my lips I have recounted all the judgements of your mouth.

14   In the path cut by your testimonies is my delight, as much as in all riches.

<sup>15</sup> May I meditate on your precepts, and may I attend to all your paths.

<sup>16</sup> In your historical statutes I shall delight myself; I shall not forget your word.

Psalm 119 is a very grand version of Psalm 25. Both psalms are written as acrostics: different kinds of ABC. Each successive verse of Psalm 25 starts with the next letter of the Hebrew alphabet; Psalm 119 has eight verses at a time, each set starting with one of those 22 letters in turn, amassing a huge 176 verses. We'll return to some of these sections in the coming days, but for now we'll concentrate on the beginning, the stanzas where the verses begin with Hebrew letters 'Aleph' and 'Beth' in turn.

Acrostics and mnemonics like this are still used today to help people learn or remember things. They might be a set of initials to prompt us – such as WWJD, 'What Would Jesus Do?', challenging us in our daily decision-making. It may be a word, like FAST, 'Face, Arms, Speech, Time', which reminds us what to do if someone has a stroke. Acrostic psalms give us a structure for our praying, our praise of God and our learning about God.

The opening verses of this longest psalm echo the spiritual use of structure. There's emphasis from the very start on walking and wandering. Two commonplace Hebrew words for 'path' are used six times in 16 verses. We are starting on a journey – but not just an abstract inner journey. This isn't the remote digital journey-planner of an impersonal navigator which we follow without thinking. This is the physical, immediate path, a city pavement or a rural bridle-way, which requires attention and isn't always clear-cut or self-explanatory. This is a walk where we are in physical contact with the ground. It's not about hopping into a car and ending up at the destination. It's about treading a way where every step counts.

The structure of the psalm maps and guides the Psalmist's wanderings. The discipline of writing thoughtful words in poetry and repeating words that begin with particular letters maintains the Psalmist's focus, keeps his soul directed to God. He is always trying to bring himself back to God, to make sure he's staying on the pathway. In meditation, and the practice of stillness, it can be so hard to keep our minds from wandering. The world is full of distractions, both around us and within. Lent is a good time to practise the discipline of bringing ourselves back to God. Anything that helps us keep this discipline is useful equipment for the journey.

Country footpaths, like those we might encounter on a few days' retreat, can be well-trodden or barely touched, helpfully signposted or overgrown. They can be a paradise of local flowers and small animals, full of delights to our senses when we stop and notice them. Psalm 119, repeatedly going back to 'the way' or 'the path', conjures up such a rural scene. Sometimes it can be good to walk free of any pre-planned agenda of our own, to let our feet take us along strange paths and discover new joys, or to find ourselves treading old familiar tracks and find rest in returning to where we've been before. Sometimes we can wander too far from the pathway, to follow a dead end, or to feel hopelessly lost with no recognizable landmark. Paths can be complicated. So can life. We need a sense of direction when we set out on a walk; we need a sense of direction in life.

We're all capable of straying from life in God. We get hopelessly caught up in what we've got to do today and don't take the time we need with God. We let other priorities take over our lives. Self-interest easily gets the better of us. We spot this in Psalm 119 too. The use of 'I' in this psalm is really striking; what the 'I' figure has done or is doing or wants is all over the place. The 'I' figure of the Psalmist is central in Psalm 119 in a way that it really isn't in other psalms. Perhaps the Psalmist learns this throughout the psalm, since in the very final verse comes the gently pathetic little comment 'I have gone astray like a sheep'.

This seems to be a 'young man' (verse 9). That fits: here is someone trying to make his way in the world, in a world where religiousness matters, where being 'righteous' counts. But how hard it is to separate being righteous from being self-righteous! Verse 14 likens the delight he can know from following a righteous path that has been cleared by God to the delight he can know in wealth. The word for wealth suggests self-sufficiency: here is someone who has gained enough that he can look after himself. The joy of dependency on God is equal to the joy of independence; the Psalmist has a way to go before he rejoices only in God and not also in his own achievements.

## Where to begin?

The disciplines of prayer, the alphabet structure, and the repeated thoughts about the 'path' – all help this young man to live his life well with God. Other literary demands in Psalm 119 hold him together too. There is a whole set of words meaning 'commandment', 'judgement', 'statute' and so on scattered with impressive evenness throughout the psalm. We see most of them already in these first two eight-verse stanzas. The Psalmist has chosen a framework that will help him reflect on some really important themes. He knows he has to keep remembering God's righteousness in all its forms. The translation above doesn't use tight equivalences between different Hebrew and English words, but chooses rather to play with what's behind them, to reflect the meditative way they are being used. The rigid framework holds the Psalmist's meandering thoughts together. The rules of composition give him a discipline to keep him on the right path.

The idea of 'keeping' – translated here in a range of different ways including 'attend to' – is also frequently expressed in Psalm 119. The psalm's discipline can 'keep' the pray-er from wandering too far from the truth. Discipline is just what a disciple, a learner, someone setting out on a journey with God, most needs. I hope the Psalms may also offer you spiritual frameworks to help you keep your Lenten disciplines.

*What helps you to keep yourself on the path towards God?*

# Friday

## ... to old

---

### Psalm 71

1   In you, O Lᴏʀᴅ, I take refuge; do not ever let me be ashamed to do so.

2   In your righteousness, snatch me away to you and help me out; lend me your ear, and save me.

3   Be to me a rocky refuge, a house that is a stronghold, to save me, because you are my high cliff and my secure place.

4   O my God, help me out of the hand of the wicked, from the clutches of the criminal and the violent,

5   for you are my absolute hope, my Lord Gᴏᴅ, my security ever since my early days.

6   Upon you have I supported myself from the womb; from my mother's belly it was you who took me. I praise you every waking moment.

7   I have become like an omen to many, but you are my mighty refuge.

8   My mouth is full of your praise, your beauty, all day and every day.

9   Do not throw me away in the time of old age; when my strength is spent, do not leave me.

10   For my enemies speak against me, and those who keep watch on my life conspire together,

11   saying, 'God has left him – pursue him and seize him! For there is no one to come to his rescue.'

12   O God, do not be distant from me! O my God, make haste to help me!

13  May *they* be the ones to be ashamed and spent, the adversaries
    of my soul; may they wrap themselves in insult and injury, those
    who want to hurt me!

14  But I, daily I shall wait in hope, and add again to all your praise.

15  My mouth will recount your righteousness every day, and
    the times you have been a saviour, even though they are
    innumerable.

16  I will come in the strengths of my Lord GOD, I shall talk about
    your righteousness, yours and only yours.

17  O God, you have taught me from my youth, and still today I
    continue to tell of your wonders.

18  So even to old age, and to grey-headedness, O God, do not
    leave me, that still I might tell of your strength to all this
    generation and all that are to come. Your greatness,

19  and your righteousness, O God, extend to the heavens above.
    The great things you have done, O God – who is there like you?

20  You, who have made me see many difficulties and evils, you
    will revive me once more; and from the deeps of the earth
    you will raise me up again.

21  May you build me up, may you continue to turn to me and
    comfort me.

22  Also, may I praise you on the best harp, for your faithfulness,
    O God; and may I make music to you on the lyre, O Holy One
    of Israel.

23  My lips will sing for joy when I make music to you; my soul
    which you have ransomed.

24  Also my tongue, all the day long, will murmur of your
    righteousness, because they are the ones who are ashamed,
    the ones who are disgraced, those who tried to wrong me.

Birthday cards feature a range of quotations about age. Often humorous, sometimes touché, occasionally cheeky, sayings about getting older are frequently about making light of old age. Getting older is something children usually celebrate, but those who are a little older often wish they could turn back the clock.

This psalm is one for those who are 'getting on a bit'. We've had the youthful confidence of Psalm 119; Psalm 71 is scattered with images of maturity. Being of a different generation, regarding oneself as 'spent', having grey hairs: this is the vulnerability that goes with 'feeling past it'. So the two psalms side by side show that the Psalter has a universal appeal. Confident worship isn't just for the young, anxious prayer isn't just for the old. They're both for everyone.

Worship and prayer are a lifelong opportunity, joy and commitment. They are about coming before God, to be oneself before God. Being oneself before God means we bring our fears and hopes, our strengths and weaknesses, our confidence, our physical and mental wobbles. God receives them all. Even the most lamenting, doubtful, frustrated, whispered prayer is a gift to God. And loud and joyful praise, even when we're facing all the struggles life throws at us, can be a gift to us.

Psalm 71 is a very vocal prayer. The sound of the human voice not only speaks the psalm, but also speaks within the text. The prayer is itself the very act of calling upon God for help. It describes spoken threats from others, and voices commitment from the self. It promises songs of praise and lessons teaching the young. The speaker's mouth, lips and tongue are instruments of God's worship, like the harp and lyre. There is a whole range of communication going on, both *to* and *about* God.

They're very realistic words too. We can probably all think of times when others have threatened us: perhaps because they're physically stronger than us, or in a position of power over us. Maybe we feel they have more say over our future than we do. Or maybe they think they are trying to help, while we think they are bullying us into life choices we don't want to make. The weaker, the more vulnerable we feel, the more we feel threatened.

That's the time we look for security. Our Psalmist today finds that security in God. God who has the strength we lack: the power to snatch us out of uncomfortable positions, the might to save us, the greatness to provide a safe refuge well away from difficult places. The picture is beautiful. God is like a sturdy house on a cliff-top, somewhere to escape to, safe and sound, a high-up hiding place.

This Lent, Psalm 71 invites us to review where our true security lies. Does it lie in ourselves, in our own vigour and strength, our achievements, the things we've built up for ourselves? Athletes rightly trust in their own bodies, muscles, strength, their hours of training; but no one can trust in those things for ever. Sometimes we *do* have to trust in others to defend us on every level – police, defence lawyers, international peacekeeping forces, loyal friends – but even the security of political or social contracts is necessarily limited.

It's hard to rely on sources of security beyond our own control; yet that is a truly inspiring source of peace in our lives. To commend ourselves, our cares and hopes, into God's hands at the end of the day is an important part of the daily monastic office of Compline, or Night Prayer. Rather than hiding in our jobs, our homes, our busyness, our hobbies, or even in our addictions, we do better to hide ourselves within God, a sure refuge during tempestuous experiences.

Think again of that language of God as a sturdy place of retreat that is high on a cliff-top. It doesn't only take courage to put our trust in something or someone other than ourselves, beyond our own sphere of influence. It's hard to look up to the heights, especially if we are bowed down. Raising our heads is something we need to remind ourselves to do. 'Looking up' is both a physical and an emotional act. We look up to gain a wider or better perspective. We see the elegance of buildings above street level. We may catch sight of future possibilities, things to look forward to.

The young are encouraged to 'raise their sights', to have aspirations. In fact, that's something we can *all* do, young or old. We might not have learnt how to aim high at all, even to think beyond the work we just fell into when we left school. But if we have learnt how to make aims, things to aim at aren't only the next job or latest possession. St Paul often writes about having goals, running races. We don't need to stop having valuable goals when we retire or even when our human frailties slow us down.

One of this Psalmist's goals is to teach a new generation about God. That's something he's never going to retire from. He doesn't want to stop teaching the wonders of his faith, the miracles of God's strong faithfulness to his people. The Psalmist just can't stop talking about that!

The Psalmist wants to carry on teaching about God: that's *his* goal. And he wants to carry on learning about God. Let's hope we too never tire of learning about God. Even when we think we've heard it all before, or we know it already. Isn't that young thing just trying to 'teach his grandmother to suck eggs'? Possibly; but we can all learn from one another about God, whether we're old, or young, or somewhere in between.

So in these early days of Lent, let's make sure we are ready to learn, ready to listen, ready to grow. Are any of us really 'grown-ups', anyway?

*How does your age matter to you?*

# Saturday

## In the beginning

———•◆•———

### Psalm 1

1   Blessed is the man who does not journey according to the advice of the wicked, who does not set himself in the path of those who do wrong, who does not inhabit the habitations of those who are derisive –

2   Rather, his delight is found in the law of the LORD, and he murmurs over that law by day and by night.

3   He is like the sapling set to root in well-watered ground: he gives fruit in due course, does not drop his leaves, and in all that he does, he thrives.

4   Not so the wicked. Rather, they are like the dust that rises from harvesting a field of grain – a gust of wind diffuses them.

5   And so the wicked will not rise to their feet in the judgement, and neither will the sinners in the gathered crowds of the righteous.

6   For the LORD knows well the way of the righteous, but the way of the wicked will die.

These first few days of Lent, we are readying ourselves to set out on our Lenten journey. So let's turn to the very beginning of the Psalter.

The Psalter was probably put together in stages. Some psalms are grouped together if they share a similar heading. That might be the somewhat intriguing title 'A psalm of ascents' – more on that later in Lent – or psalms attributed to a particular author, like Asaph.

There are also bigger collections. The Psalms have been arranged into five different 'books'. Psalms 1–41 are the first book. (The other four books run 42–72; 73–89; 90–106; 107–150. If you look at

Psalms 41, 72, 89, 106 and 150 you'll find they close with a doxology, a formula of praise, indicating the end of a section.)

So the Psalter grew up in dribs and drabs; the way we see it today is the end product of a long process of editing, and careful arrangement and rearrangement. Psalms 1 and 2 were added later, placed at the very beginning of the collection as an introduction.

Psalm 1 sets the tone: this teaches wisdom. The very first word, 'Blessed', is a word sometimes translated 'Happy', meaning the one who is at peace in life, who is good at dealing with whatever life throws up. It's about a fundamental stabilizing happiness, or joy. This is the kind of person who has the deep inner strength to face things well.

He cannot be distracted from the right way of doing life. And verse 6 makes clear, as in Psalm 119, that it is precisely about a 'way'.

In John's Gospel, Jesus says, 'I am the way, the truth, and the life' (John 14.6). 'The way' is important to Jesus. It's a rich theological theme. There's the way through the wilderness, the way to God, the way of the cross and so on. Each of us is a journeyer through life.

Psalm 1 explores where we place ourselves. The first few words about journeying are replaced by verbs that are more about settling. The hero of the illustration goes from not 'journeying' with the wicked, via not 'standing' with them, to not 'sitting' with them. Each leads to the next. If we fall in with wrongdoers, we risk staying with them, sticking with them always, says the Psalmist. What we should do instead is make sure that we stick with God's guidance in all things, God's *torah*.

The next picture shows this beautifully. Rather than following those who might lead us astray, we should settle down like young trees that are transplanted, saplings growing their roots deep beside life-giving streams of water. Then our journey is not at risk of going off the rails, but rather grows profoundly. Then we can be fruitful and vibrant.

At the very outset of the Psalter, like young saplings, we have potential. Like those beginning a journey, we have choices to make. Where do we put ourselves ready to set out? Where do we want to go? Do we want to let ourselves be swept along with whatever crowd we fall into? Do we want to let ourselves be planted in a well-watered place, where we can tap into deep resources to help us flourish?

The Psalmist invites us to do the last of these. Then we can grow up, grow hardy and substantial. He compares this process in verse 4 with the wicked who are like an insubstantial cloud of dust, literally dissipated. These countryside images crammed into the opening verses are wide-ranging and attractive. We skip from one poetic painting to the next. Each of them combines raw natural beauty with careful stewardship. There is the path that is well kept; the sapling that is transplanted for the sake of its own nurture; the ground that is well watered because of the irrigation channels hinted at by the Hebrew vocabulary; the dust that is produced by the harvester.

In verse 5 the rural suddenly gives place to the law court. It's threatening at first glance. No one wants to find himself face to face with people who are bringing charges or giving testimony against him, let alone get caught up in those very crowds. But the Psalmist is reassuring. Verse 6 says that because the wicked are dissipated, they have no strength to do this; like clouds of dust they really don't have a leg to stand on, we might say. It is the righteous who have buried their roots deep whose journey through life will be protected by God.

So we are to be deeply rooted in God in order to journey through life. Who knows who else might lead us astray? The word for 'wicked' recurs many times both in Psalm 1 and in the rest of the Psalter. It is a kind of 'anti-type', an example to avoid. There are lots of different ways to translate it, to help it resonate with our experience today. 'The wicked' sometimes seems a little abstract, disjointed from our daily life. It's not a word we see often in newspapers. So what, or who, really are 'the wicked' or 'the wrongdoers'? What we notice in our Lenten journey of penitence is that we can easily fall into those ways ourselves. At the beginning of the journey we should check out what direction we want to head in, what company we might want to keep, and even what kind of company we might be for those around us.

*Think of someone whose company does you good. What is it about that person that makes his or her company such a gift?*

# WEEK 1

It's a hard world

# Monday

## Friends and enemies

---

### Psalm 55

1   To the music director. To music: a song of understanding, of
    David.
2   I implore you, O God, hear my prayer: do not hide yourself
    from my plea for favour.
3   Give me your full attention, and answer me; I rove in my
    ruminations,
4   because of the noise of the enemy, faced with the wicked
    pressing upon me. For they make trouble tumble down upon
    me, and in anger they continue to hold grudges against me.
5   My heart thumps in my chest, and the terrors of death have
    fallen upon me.
6   Fear and trembling lodge in my gut, and I am shaking from
    head to toe.
7   And I say, 'Who will give me the wings of a dove? Let me fly
    away, and settle there –
8   yes,' I say, 'let me retreat far away, let me make my lodging in
    the wilderness. *Selah.*
9   Let me hurry to a place that is safe for me, out of the rushing
    wind and the storm.'
10  O Lord, drown their voices, make them argue – for I see
    violence and strife in the city.
11  Day and night they tour its walls, and woe and trouble lie deep
    within it.
12  Ruin lies at its heart; injustice and deceit never leave its main
    square.

13   For it is not actually an enemy who is being sharp with me – for then I could make sense of it; it is not someone who hates me who is puffing himself up against me – for then I could hide myself away from him.

14   It is you – someone just like me, someone who is my friend, someone I know well –

15   you and I together used to enjoy good conversation, in God's Temple we used to walk together in the crowd.

16   May death pay them back, may they go down to the grave alive; for evil is in their homes and in their hearts.

17   As for me, let me call upon God, and the Lord will save me.

18   Evening, morning, and noontime I sigh and moan; he hears my voice.

19   He redeems my soul in peace from the fight against me, even though there are many against me.

20   God hears and answers them, he who has been on the throne for ages past. *Selah.*
    He has an answer for those who refuse to change, those who have no respect for God.

21   That so-called friend set his hands against me, he desecrated his relationship with me.

22   Buttery is his smooth speech, but fighting is in his heart. His words are softer than oil, but they are in fact drawn swords.

23   Cast upon the Lord all you have been given, and he will support you; he does not forever give such a shaking to the righteous.

24   But you, O God, will bring them down to the deepest pit. Men of blood and deceit will not live to middle age. It is in you that I put my trust.

This psalm is best known as 'O, for the wings of a dove' – a beautiful, yearning song written by Mendelssohn. The German Romantic composer set all of verses 2–8 to music, although the memorable solo usually sung by a young chorister consists only of verses 7–8. I've offered a slightly different translation of these well-known verses because when something seems familiar, we can be lulled into a sense that we know what it's all about. But do we really?

The famous prayer for the wings of a dove merely hints at the elemental emotions expressed throughout the whole prayer. These are such gut-wrenching feelings because they result from the worst kind of betrayal.

The first section of the psalm – Mendelssohn's choice – describes the terror of facing an enemy. The physical, bodily reactions of the Psalmist, caught in the grip of fear, are vividly depicted. In verses 5 and 6 he's sharing an experience of a contemporary 'panic attack'. Ruminating is something we do when we're down, when we find we can't stop worrying about something, restlessly going over it again and again. He's literally feeling overwhelmed by things falling down about him. He's showing some of the deep symptoms of anxiety.

What does the Psalmist do with all this? He prays. Hard.

We probably all know only too well what this kind of experience can feel like – how we feel stuck, trapped, afraid, and want a quick, easy escape. That then is why the Psalmist prays so fervently for the wings of a dove. In his imagination he escapes far away, to a space of solitude.

He gains some distance in this way, and is able to look upon things with a more detached perspective. It's only then that he can describe what's going on in the city, in his home. There's violence, strife, every kind of deceit and treachery. The very worst kind of treachery, that which inspires such hefty emotions, is the betrayal perpetrated by a friend.

It has taken more than half the psalm for this heartbreaking truth to come out. Verse 14 begins with the turning point 'It is you'.

Up to this point, the Psalmist has been addressing God. Now he changes focus, and we learn that the new addressee is someone just like the Psalmist, someone he knows well. His best friend. His soul-mate.

After addressing his former friend for two verses, the Psalmist can face him no more. He looks again at depersonalized enemies, nameless foes, the abstract form of this very concrete individual. It's not pretty.

Such is his hurt, his bitterness, that he curses his old friend as hard as he can. He wishes the worst kind of end upon him. That's what he deserves, says the Psalmist. That's what he's worth.

After this outburst of vitriolic anger, his tone suddenly changes. Now he describes his own holiness and relationship with God: how he praises him, trusts in him, calls upon him. Consequently, he says, God will redeem him, however many enemies he faces.

This changing of focus, between God and his old companion, goes along with a vast wavering through the rest of the psalm. Thinking about God's faithfulness is steadying; thinking about his faithless friend makes him veer towards violence. The relationships couldn't be more contrasting. The former soul-mate has made this friendship filthy. God's lasting covenant relationship is unbroken and cleansing.

That's the story. That's why the Psalmist wants to get out of here. He can't face it any longer. He can't face the fact that he is surrounded by those who want to do him harm. He can't face his friend any more. Perhaps he can't even face the fact that being betrayed in this way has led him to such vicious feelings towards his old companion. There is a two-way betrayal here: the former best mate may have been the first to break that friendship, but the Psalmist now heaps curses upon him as if he himself never knew him.

How do you respond when you realize you didn't truly know someone you thought you understood inside out? When the person you thought you could trust above everyone else shows herself to be worse than the lot of them?

It shakes us to the core. There's lots of language of shaking in this prayer: shaking because of unsteadiness; shaking because of fear, anxiety. God is an antidote to such shakiness. When we realize that a relationship is not as we thought it was, it shakes our very foundations. We doubt who we ourselves are; we doubt who we thought we were. We might blame ourselves. We might, like the Psalmist, wholeheartedly blame the other.

A friend's betrayal means she no longer deserves to be called a friend. Worse still, she must be an enemy, because we have been labouring for so long in false belief in her. That's the crux of the Psalmist's anger and why he is so gutted: he's just realized that his best friend is *now* his enemy, and so effectively *has been all along*.

A friend's betrayal finds its place in the Passion narrative too: Judas Iscariot's betrayal of Jesus, even with a kiss – that spine-tingling moment as the deed is done through the most intimate sign of friendship. Yet, unlike the wronged Psalmist, we don't hear Jesus piling insults or curses on Judas. Perhaps that's one reason why Judas can no longer bear himself: because Jesus in that moment of betrayal just longed to have his friend back.

We've all been betrayed, or we've betrayed others. When you've been betrayed, have you responded more like the Psalmist, or like Jesus? When you've betrayed someone, have you wanted that person to be angry with you, or forgive you?

Above all, when we're most shaken up, do we lean on God?

*Think of someone you would rather avoid. How might you offer that person, that relationship, to God?*

# Tuesday

## *The pain of loss*

———•◆•———

### Psalm 74

1 A song of understanding, of Asaph.
   Why, O God, do you perpetually reject us? Why does your
   anger smoke against the flock in your pastoral care?
2 Remember the congregation you procured long ago, the
   people you redeemed as your heirs, this Mount Zion where
   you settled.
3 Direct your footsteps up to the perpetual ruins, all that the foe
   has destroyed in the sanctuary.
4 Your enemies have roared in the very midst of your special
   place, they have put their signs all over it.
5 You could recognize them – they were those who brought
   to the upper gate axes like they would use to chop down a
   thicket of trees.
6 And now, its collection of engravings, they hack at these with
   hatchet and pike.
7 They made your sanctuary go up in flames, to the ground they
   desecrated the place where your name dwells.
8 They said to themselves, 'Let us completely crush them!' They
   burnt all the meeting-places of God in the land.
9 Our ensigns, we can no longer see them; no prophet is left;
   there is no one who knows how long this will go on for.
10 How long will the foe be so sharp with us? Will the enemy
   scorn your name for ever more?
11 Why do you hold back your hand, even your right hand? From
   your breast draw it out and finish them!

12 Yet God is my King from of old, he works salvation throughout the land.

13 You, by your might, split open the sea; you shattered the heads of the sea-monsters in the waters.

14 You, you crushed the heads of Leviathan, and you gave him as food to the throng of wild beasts.

15 You, you broke open spring and torrent; you, you dried up ever-flowing rivers.

16 Yours is the day, yours also is the night; you, you fixed in space the moon and the sun.

17 You, you set up all the boundaries of the earth: summer and winter, you, you created them.

18 Remember this: the enemy has scorned you, Lord, and foolish people have spurned your name.

19 Do not hand over the soul of your dove to the wild beast! Do not forget the life of your oppressed people for ever!

20 Pay attention to your covenant! For the dark corners of the earth are full of places where violence makes its home.

21 Let not the oppressed turn away, humiliated: let the poor and needy praise your name!

22 Rise up, O God, defend your own case! Remember how you are scorned by the foolish all day long!

23 Do not forget the shout of the enemy, the din of those who stand against you, which goes up continually.

When we're having a tough time, it feels as though it's going to go on for ever. We simply can't see how things will ever improve: we're stuck, low, disheartened. There is no light at the end of the tunnel.

The loss of someone (or something) dear to us is like that. We don't just lose a beloved person, place, job or ability. We lose much more besides. We lose our former ideas about the world, about life, about our own identity. Our perspective is changed irrecoverably. We lose hope, even losing any hope that we can ever hope again.

Yesterday, we thought about the loss of a relationship, and what that loss can look like. The beloved can even become someone who riles us, changed from friend to enemy. Someone who brought pleasure and joy now brings pain, bitter anger. Today, Psalm 74 describes the loss of a place, the loss of a way of life and holiness that defines people. It goes so far as the loss of God himself. It's no surprise that it's bleak.

Some psalms perhaps have origins reaching back as far as the late second millennium, but the dates of many are greatly debated. However, Psalm 74 is usually associated with an historical event which we *can* date, namely the loss of the First Temple at the fall of Jerusalem in 586 BC. The Babylonians, under King Nebuchadnezzar II, had already been attacking Jerusalem for almost 20 years. In 605 BC, Nebuchadnezzar's power had been on the rise, and Judah was the next target in his battle plan. He invaded, but left the city of Jerusalem standing because he was given money in taxes, valuables, and royal or noble hostages (including Daniel the prophet). A few years later, Judah rebelled and stopped paying these taxes, so Nebuchadnezzar besieged Jerusalem, which fell for the first time in 597 BC. Nebuchadnezzar withdrew, looting the Temple, taking the king, aristocracy, officers and craftsmen into exile. The now puppet city rebelled again in 587 BC and the subsequent siege by the Babylonians completely destroyed both the city and the Temple. Many more were now deported from Jerusalem to Babylon, and only a handful of the poorest were left in their ruined city.

So Jerusalem, Mount Zion, and the very dwelling place of God, the Temple itself (which had been built by King Solomon), are lost. Judah is lost. The exiles are lost. The king is lost. With all this, the Psalmist's faith is severely tested.

When our faith is shaken to the foundations by whatever life throws at us, it's good to know that prayers are out there for such a dread moment. Ancient, well-worn prayers give us company in our distress. The Psalms are living texts which we can use, and use again; we, and many others all across the world.

Repeating words such as 'for ever', 'perpetually', 'continually', Psalm 74 resonates with all human experiences of loss, even loss of faith. Momentary glimpses of the destruction of Jerusalem are like freeze-frames or flashbacks. They speak of trauma, of the pain of watching something beloved and integral to an understanding of life crumble before us. Those moments feel as though they could go on for ever; we think the images printed in our mind's eye will last perpetually. A moment becomes an eternity. The Psalmist makes readers like us throughout the generations look at those pictures of desecration and ruin along with him.

As these images reflect something of our own stories of loss and bereavement, so we are in company with others for whom the narrative of Psalm 74 also rings true. We are not alone in our loss; it is an inescapable part of our humanity. Where there is growth, there is change; where there is change, there is loss.

Children today are frequently said to be 'growing up too quickly', to be 'losing their innocence'. As we grow older and wiser, we too continue to lose our innocence. What we're watching in Psalm 74 is the Psalmist's loss of innocence. This place, this sanctuary he thought impregnable because it was the house of God's own name, God's might, God's power, is brought down piece by piece with rudimentary tools and weapons. The Psalmist stands and watches, helpless; and wonders if God too is standing watching, helpless . . . Surely God must have turned his face away, for he is mighty and strong to save, so he would not put up with such destruction of his dwelling place. The Psalmist tries to bring God's attention back to this life-changing moment, with pleas and commands.

Again there is a turning point. Halfway through, the Psalmist utters the astonishingly upbeat words: 'Yet God is my King from of old, he works salvation throughout the land.' The next verses are a wonderful, faithful whistle-stop tour proclaiming how God is Lord of creation. He has power over even the most terrifying of creatures; he himself created all the earth. Is this excursion into creation a digression, a means of escapism?

No – for two reasons. First, because this personal reminder of the greatness of God helps to shore up the Psalmist's faith, and so helps us too to go back to the foundations of our faith in moments of crisis. It helps the Psalmist in the following verses to cry out all the more powerfully to God: 'Remember!' 'Pay attention!' 'Do not forget . . .!' All these are cries to God which speak of a trust that hands all things over to God, and throws despair and desolation at God. The very act of praying, whatever the tone, is a sign that hope still flickers. Second, because the Hebrew word for 'salvation' is 'Yeshua', and that's the name of Jesus. Joshua, Jesus: these related names are about deliverance and salvation, being saved. Yearning for salvation, hoping for Jesus: these are one and the same thing, one word with deep and ancient roots. Praying this psalm today, we remember Jesus, the hope of salvation which may sometimes flicker, but never goes out.

*What would you most like God to remember?*

# Wednesday
## Wilderness and loneliness

———————

## Psalm 63

1  A song of David, when he was in the wilderness of Judah.

2  O God, you are my God, I look out for you early each morning. My soul is thirsty for you, my flesh yearns for you, as in a dry and fainting land where the water has run out.

3  Just like this have I looked upon you in your sanctuary, seeing your power and your glory.

4  Because your love is better even than life, my lips shall praise you.

5  And so I shall bless you as long as I live; in your name I shall lift up my hands.

6  As at a sumptuous feast, my soul will be satisfied; with joyful lips my mouth will praise you,

7  when I remember you on my bed, and meditate on you during the hours of night.

8  For you have been my helper, and under the shadow of your wings I will shout with joy.

9  My soul clings on to you, and your right hand grasps me.

10  But those who want to destroy my soul, they will go down to the depths of the earth.

11  They will be given over to the power of the sword; they shall become food for jackals.

12  But the king shall rejoice in God, all those who take oaths in his name will praise him, because the mouth of anyone who speaks lies shall be shut up.

We've landed firmly in the first week of Lent, and have already experienced two poignant laments from the Psalms. Psalm 63 is less full of angst but still high in emotion, speaking beautifully of prayer in solitude.

Psalm 55 yearned for the wilderness. Now we're there. Perhaps you were looking forward to Lent, to stripping things back to basics, simplifying your life and making the light burden of Jesus your priority. Perhaps you've been hoping to declutter from material things or frantic busy-ness, and now you're getting going. If you're like me, you'll have had many good intentions to be more 'holy', but may not have managed it yet. So – even if we are struggling to make the space in our lives for God as we started planning to do this Lent – let's enter that space imaginatively.

For that is what the Psalmist is doing here. Are we in the wilderness? The first line suggests it, but this is another of those superscriptions, headings that may have been added later. It rings true at first: this is a dry and fainting land, a landscape that is barren and unforgiving. That gasping for water pictures the Psalmist's gasping for God. This is energetic devotion, a commitment to God that takes over the whole of the Psalmist, body and soul.

Suddenly, we're in the Temple. In verse 3 the Psalmist relives a memory of worship, of a religious experience in the Jerusalem sanctuary, the place where God's glory and power were believed to reside. This relationship with God makes the Psalmist full of praise. Even in the wilderness he joins remotely in the holy words and actions of the Temple.

In the next two verses this vision slips away, just like a dream. The Psalmist is alone, praying, on his bed. That image too makes sense. In children's literature a generation or two ago, the idea that you'd kneel beside your bed and say your prayers before going to sleep was common. Now we may be surprised to visit a friend's house and hear her saying her prayers with her child after reading the bedtime story.

Praying at bedtime works. I mentioned Compline, or Night Prayer, while thinking in Psalm 71 about letting God be in control. A simple, short collection of prayers and readings, this really can help to put the day to bed. 'Into your hands, O Lord, I commend my spirit.' We commend into God's hands today's joys, successes, fail-ures, the people we've spent time with, the people and things we have been worrying about all day long. We can't do anything more about it right now. So it's best to let God give us sleep (just as he wants to give us rest in Psalms 4 and 127).

The bed is a good place for dreaming . . . Like the Psalmist we travel in our imagination; we can experience special holy places even when we can't get there. The seventeenth-century bishop Jeremy Taylor wrote: 'There should be in the soul halls of space, avenues of leisure, and high porticos of silence, where God walks.' Entering an inner space where we can meet with God is often more realistic than finding time for a good long walk, taking a retreat or visiting a pilgrimage site.

It's in that inner space that the Psalmist meets with God. This is also an opportunity to remember places where he has had special moments with God: the sanctuary and joyful worship; the great spaciousness of the wilderness where the majesty of the Creator is awe-inspiring.

Spiritual moments go on feeding us, whether we remember them privately or talk about them with others. Retreats can be times of peace, joy, and all the real and simple basics of life and prayer. Life elsewhere can be complicated and hurried. Remembering a retreat can be almost as good as being there. Entering a contemplative space in our imagination is an immense gift: that of God-focused day-dreaming. Like praying with an icon and letting ourselves spiritually enter that divine frame. Like the practice of *lectio divina*, when we enter imaginatively into the Bible story we are meditating upon.

Solitude gives us space for inner wanderings of heart, mind and spirit. Being still on our beds, we can drink in the presence of God. We can recall occasions when we've met with him, and when we've been fed by him. We can relive times when we have felt at one with God. We re-member, piece back together again, the peace and joy we have known, and confidently look forward to similar holy, life-giving moments we will experience in future.

So the actual setting of this prayer doesn't matter. Whether this is wilderness remembering of comfortable holy solitude, or noisy exciting church worship, or home-alone contemplation, it doesn't matter. What matters is that we can meet with God anywhere; we can store up those experiences; we can call them to mind. If I'm feeling stressed, I might imagine broad horizons, open skies and a peaceful spacious heart. If I'm feeling low, I might recall the chapel where I come together with a local community of Franciscans, and the life-giving vows I took in their company.

Different people experience loneliness for different reasons. The fragile patient in a nursing home; the students shy at socializing; the recently bereaved; those who have just moved homes or jobs or had some other major life change. High responsibility, 'being at the top', can bring loneliness; so can the isolation of illness or addiction.

Sometimes, though, it might be possible to relish loneliness as solitude, silence as gift, personal space as liberating.

No matter how alone we feel, God is with us.

*What helps you most when you feel lonely?*

# Thursday
## Exile and war

---

## Psalm 120

1  A song of ascents. To the Lᴏʀᴅ I cried in my distress, and he
   answered me.
2  'O Lᴏʀᴅ, deliver my soul from lying lips, from a deceitful tongue!
3  You deceitful tongue, what will be given to you, and what will
   you gain?
4  This: a warrior's arrows, sharpened over the hottest charcoal!
5  Oh, I can't carry on much longer: for I have stayed a while with
   Meshech, and I have lived in the tents of Kedar.
6  For too long has my soul lived with those who hate peace and
   good!
7  I am all for peace; but when I speak, they want to fight!'

There's always someone to pray for, always a part of the world to call
to mind in our prayers, whether those repeated in church or those
we say privately. There are famines, epidemics and natural disasters;
wars and rumours of wars; lawlessness, suffering and great distress.
This little list looks suspiciously like what Jesus predicted in the
so-called 'Little Apocalypse' detailed in both Mark's and Matthew's
Gospels. The end times are always on the horizon. The world needs
our prayers.

Psalm 120 spans a range of strife in just seven verses. Deceit, fraud,
weapons, despair, weariness, homeless wanderings, hatred, fighting . . . The combination of images and language points to humanity's fight for survival, greed for personal profit, and the directionless
journeying associated with human migration or the flight of refugees. Whose words are these anyway?

35

That's one of the questions put to us most keenly by this psalm. It's nearly all direct speech. It's the quotation of a prayer, a prayer-within-a-prayer. 'To the LORD I cried in my distress' in verse 1 introduces the next six verses, the whole of the rest of the psalm. This is a prayer from the heart caught on paper.

When I'm in difficulty, I sometimes find it hard to pray. That's when I most need other people's prayers. It's not so much a list of requests to God on my behalf for things to get better for me that I'm looking for; instead, I need other people to do my praying for me. At theological college, for instance, seeing some votive candles glowing, I found comfort in the very possibility that a friend might have lit one for me. I was struggling to say my own prayers; I needed someone else to enter that prayer space with God on my behalf. All I felt able to do was stand on the sidelines of my own prayer and hope someone else might say the words of the prayers for me, have the intentions of prayer for me.

The book of Psalms as a whole has something to say about this: here are ready-made prayers, tried and tested prayers, prayers where the hard work has already been done. When we're praying them, we do so not only with our Christian brothers and sisters throughout the world, but with our Jewish brothers and sisters, and with generations of all nationalities past and present who have used them for their own devotions and in their public worship. Talk about a community of saints! It's the same with all prepared liturgy. Others, prayerful, careful people, have done the theology for us, the hard thinking about what words might just be the right ones at this moment. We don't have to reinvent the wheel. We simply have to rest upheld in other people's prayer lives.

This prayer in particular, with its range of voices and vocabulary, reminds us to pray others' prayers for them. It's likely we will have come face to face with people who have deceived us, at work or at home; that we in turn have deceived others, whether intentionally or not. We will have come across people who are in it for their own gain, who want to profit at any cost; and we've probably ourselves sometimes put our own desires above other people's needs. We can understand the barely veiled anger and frustration at people who have lied or been manipulative. This might be our own prayer, or a prayer we make on behalf of others who are presently having that experience.

If we've had to move around a lot, or if our neighbourhood just isn't very neighbourly, we may be able to empathize with a lifestyle that does not feel rooted in a place or community. Such a situation isn't life-giving. We notice what we are missing whenever we do experience true community, like a happy institution or a thriving monastic house. We can understand the world-weariness engendered when we don't truly belong in a place or society. Psalm 120 could even be the prayer of our brothers and sisters who are couch-surfing with friends, a few nights here, a few there, because they've got nowhere else to go. Verse 5 is open to all sorts of different plights, from dislocation to the extreme poverty of homelessness. Here we have a prayer that can resonate both with our own circumstances and with the heavy sigh of many others, even in our own streets, whose circumstances we can't begin to understand.

There's a desire for peaceful coexistence expressed in verses 6 and 7. Again, we might know on an intimate, domestic scale the desire to get on well with colleagues or next-door neighbours, or our teenage daughter or son's new girlfriend or boyfriend. We might know what strife can be experienced in stressed-out family existence, or in a work-place under extreme pressure, where disagreement echoes through meeting rooms and corridors. But many of us are fortunate enough not to be living in a war zone, where bullets ricochet off nearby pock-marked buildings at all hours, or explosions distant or close at hand send out smoke or shockwaves. We can barely imagine what that must be like. Once again we can make this prayer our own, and we can also make it a prayer for others whose lives are distant from our own.

The Psalms, handed down through millennia, invite us to make them our own, and require us to make them our prayers for the world. Yesterday we thought about reimagining, through prayer places, moments where we encountered God. Today, effectively, we do the same: with prayer that calls to mind images of people who are in the midst of some kind of exile or war. There too we encounter God.

*What kind of pictures come to mind when you think of exile and war, and how do you pray about them?*

# Friday
## Without hope

---

## Psalm 88

1 A song. A psalm of the sons of Korah. For the Director of Music: to the tune Song in Affliction (Mahalath Leannoth). A song of understanding, of Heman the Ezrahite.

2 O LORD, God who saves me, I have cried out day and night before you.

3 Let my prayer come to your face; bend your ear to my cry!

4 For full of troubles is my soul, and my whole life reaches to hell.

5 I am reckoned like those who are going down to the imprisoning earth; I am become a man who has no help left.

6 Among the dead I have been let go; like the fatally wounded lying in the grave: you remember them no longer and they are cut off from your hand.

7 You have put me in the lowest part of the confining grave, in places dark and deep.

8 Your rage bears down on me; all your breakers overwhelm me. *Selah*.

9 You have made my friends keep their distance from me; you have made me an appalling sight to them; I am confined so that I cannot get out.

10 My eyes grow weary because of my affliction; I call to you, O LORD, all day long, I stretch my hands to you.

11 Surely you don't work wonders for the dead? Surely those who are dead and gone don't rise up to praise you? *Selah*.

12 Surely neither your steadfast love is recounted in the grave, nor your faithfulness in the extremes of hell?

13 Surely neither your wonders are made known in the darkness, nor your righteous works in the land where all is forgotten?

14 As for me . . . to you, O LORD, I cry for help, and each morning my prayer greets you.

15 Why, O LORD, do you reject my soul? Why do you hide your face from me?

16 Wretched and dying – ever since my early life – I have borne your terrors! I am helpless.

17 Over me have swept your burning angers, your terrors are the end of me!

18 They surround me like the waters all the day long; they close in upon me on every side.

19 You have put far from me those who used to love me and be my friends; those known to me have left me in darkness.

Psalm 88 is the most wretched of all the psalms. Other psalms of heavy despair offer some glimmer of hope, even if only at the end. But there is apparently nothing heartening here at all. All is desperate, desolate, darkness.

We might associate this psalm with the night of Jesus' arrest. If you've been to the Holy Land, perhaps you have visited the remains of what is believed to be the high priest's house in Jerusalem at the time of Jesus. Whether or not this was the exact place where Jesus was imprisoned on the night before his crucifixion matters less than what it helps us learn about those few hours. You can visit chambers beneath the house which would have been used as a primitive prison: pits dug out deep underground, some deeper than others, from which there was no escape.

Such a prison was used for those, like Jesus, who were awaiting trial. It was a trial and a punishment in itself. Alone, isolated in the pitch blackness, it would be easy to imagine you'd been buried alive and would just be left there to die. A prison, a grave . . . in a sense there would be little difference between the two. In such a helpless situation, death would seem like your only companion.

Today these prisons, the so-called 'Pit', or cisterns (for sometimes they might also have contained water), are well-lit venues on a pilgrim trail. But even now, to read or sing Psalm 88 in these places is chilling. The setting makes sense of the language through-out the psalm of 'hell' in different forms, of the grave, confinement, the waters, depths, darkness and imminent death, of being alone and apart from anyone who was once a friend or relative.

Could this really have been how Jesus spent some of his hours between Gethsemane and his trial? Could these words really have been used by Jesus, the rabbi so well versed in Hebrew Scripture that he could find the right prayer for any occasion?

This picture helps us imagine ourselves into the kind of place envisaged in the psalm, and the many metaphors of darkness and death that we can tap into today. This is a nearly unthinkable situation where hope itself is simply impossible to imagine: Death Row, torture by waterboarding, the deepest solitary confinement, some-thing that feels as though it will go on for ever – until death itself, that is. Whether or not it was the prayer Jesus himself prayed that night, it could have been the prayer of many a Jew in imprisonment before Jesus' day, and indeed after.

To read it as a prayer used by Jesus himself adds meaning to Christ's Passion. Thinking of him imprisoned like this makes his suf-fering and trial more concrete. It invites us to consider him experi-encing the deepest of darknesses, contemplating an unknown, silent, even God-forsaken death. Just as friends, relatives, companions, seem uncompromisingly unreachable, so even does God.

And yet . . . the basic action of a prayer like this brings a glimpse of hope:

*So, God can't hear me. But what if there's a tiny chance that he can? I'll keep praying, come what may.*

Then it gets darker.

*So if there's even a chance God can hear me, why does he ignore me?*

Now that's despair indeed. The text closes in complete darkness, just like the Pit. Where's the hope in that?

Well, the hope lies in the very existence of a text like this, the fact that it's been handed down through generation after generation means it has value. Others have valued it. They have survived to tell the tale. The text has survived: so will we. The prayer has gone on: so will our relationship with God. Despite *all this.*

Isolation is pictured in the text. The text itself, though, speaks beyond that isolation. We are here to read it. Different people have prayed it. Life may be desperate, but even now we are not alone, we will not be alone. Others have been in this Pit before us. Others will be in it after us. Others have needed to pray this psalm. Others will feel moved to do so. The very fact that it continues to be read and prayed means that it goes on being heard.

The rhetorical questions of verses 11–13 in one sense expect the answer 'Of course not. Of course the dead cannot praise God!' In another sense, they expect no answer at all: they cannot be heard . . . And yet, in the light of Christ, we can defy these expectations, this utter hopelessness. We can answer them. Better, we can even answer them with the completely unexpected answer.

'Yes, God does work wonders for the dead! Yes, those who are dead and gone, even they can rise up and praise God!'

Jesus gives us the light in that darkness. He gives the unexpected answers. He *is* the astounding answer.

More than that, his own utter darkness is our answer. Whether through this text or through our reading of the Passion narratives, we see it's possible that even Jesus himself knew the fullest darkness, the deepest despair. We don't need to beat ourselves up about having times of despair and darkness: that is not a lack of faith, neither are we getting something wrong that we should correct ourselves. It is just a part of the human, mortal condition. We can know hopelessness. So could Jesus.

Even that hopelessness couldn't confine Jesus, and it can't confine us. 'Nothing can separate us from the love of God that is in Christ Jesus' (Romans 8). This is lived out in Psalm 88, in these very cisterns; and in the deepest, darkest corners of our own lives.

*How does it feel to think of God touching even the very darkest corners of your life?*

# Saturday

## Without God, without goodness

---

## Psalm 53

¹ To the Director of Music: Tone Mahalath. A song of
understanding, of David.

² The foolish man says in his heart, 'There is no God!' They are
ruined and they act abominably. Not one of them does good.

³ God from heaven looks out across the sons of Adam to see if
there is anyone alive who understands, who seeks God in the
study of his word.

⁴ Each one is a backslider, all together they are corrupt, there is
simply no one, not one, who does good.

⁵ Are they entirely stupid, those who do evil, those who eat away
at my people as if they are eating bread, and do not call upon
God?

⁶ There, they shall be struck down with terror, and never was
there a terror like it!
For God will tear apart limb by limb the one who entrenches
himself against you; you put them to shame because God has
rejected them.

⁷ If only the salvation of Israel would come from Zion! When
God turns his people to return to him, let Jacob rejoice, let
Israel exult!

'It's a hard world': this week we've looked over some psalms which
vividly capture that sentiment. Now the Psalmist peers with God at
the evildoer, the atheist, and hopes so strongly that such people are
going to meet a bad end that it's as if it has already happened.

The practical atheist here lives life entirely without God, spurning wholeheartedly what others call by that name. Defence against such people is so entrenched that almost this entire psalm is found in Psalm 14 too. This was a rationale that was important and consequently widespread. The two psalms differ only in two real respects. First, the name that is used for God: probably an early, common form of the text travelled to different areas where different people made it their own. Second, 53.6 is a more vicious version of the softer, more positive Psalm 14.5–6. This was a well-rehearsed theme: the angry bad behaviour of the atheist towards the holy, and the atheist's eventual comeuppance.

That can be a comfort to us today. Unless we have surrounded ourselves solely with religious friends, we all know people who disdain God, Jesus, organized religion, or belief systems. It can be hard to live or work alongside people who disrespect our faith, whether openly or more secretly.

We should all be able to speak about our belief systems, whatever faith or no-faith defines us. What we can all do without, though, is the anger that sometimes goes along with religious or anti-religious assertions. 'Are all atheists angry?' is a common question. Whatever the answer, such anger is liable to spread, and that doesn't help anyone.

'Without God, without goodness': this summary of verse 2 risks slipping into a mindset which says 'Christian good, secularist bad'; or, in our multicultural society, 'someone with faith is good, someone without faith bad'. It's not that simple.

We must always be willing to let our faith be honed, refined, challenged, thereby letting it grow. We might have a strong faith already, but our God is always bigger than we can wholly grasp. We need to be continually 'on our mettle': ready to encounter God in ways we'd never thought of before. Sometimes we can meet God in the most astonishing of places and people. The Franciscan friary in Dorset in its welcome leaflet describes meeting with other people who are different from ourselves: 'Try to see Christ's face in them, never do anything to hurt them, and listen to them until you are able to discern the flame that burns in each person.'

Although, along with Psalm 14, we might want to rant about atheists, we need to think more delicately, even tenderly, about those who differ from us. It's not helpful for us today to say 'Are they really *that* stupid?' (verse 5), to lump together everyone who doesn't believe like we do, or to go as far as thinking wishfully of their destruction. They are our brothers and sisters, like it or not.

Atheism can make our world hard. Perhaps we're fighting to wear a cross at work, or perhaps someone's subtly bullying us and what we stand for. But our struggles in our increasingly secularized society are as nothing in comparison to those who really are being persecuted for their faith. There are people who are daily severely persecuted as Christians. Along with the ancient saints, our church calendars remember recent martyrs like Dietrich Bonhoeffer, Janani Luwum, Oscar Romero, Brother Roger of Taizé, Jacques Hamel. Those religious persecutions we hear about on the news are perhaps just the tip of the iceberg. Then the words of Psalm 53 ring true, when it speaks of those who eat up God's people as if they were eating bread, those who act abominably because of their own religious or anti-religious standpoint. We should yearn for justice for those who are oppressed for their faith.

Yet we also have a responsibility to the other. A responsibility, yes, to those who share our faith, such that we pray for them, stand up for them, help them practically if ever we can. But also a responsibility to those who are of a different mindset. Jesus tells us to love our enemies and pray for those who persecute us. That's hard to do.

I tell you, though, miracles can happen. Even for the most raging atheist or the most dogmatic person of one faith or another.

I'm often asked: 'Is the God of the Old Testament the same as the God of the New Testament?' Certainly, setting Psalm 53 against the sayings of Jesus does highlight some of the differences. It also reminds us how much further we have to go. Jesus didn't stop with the Hebrew Scriptures; he immersed himself in them, learned them backwards, developed new and living ways of applying them. Perhaps this is the true 'song of understanding' that our Lenten journey through the Psalms will help us sing.

Is there 'anyone alive who understands, who seeks God in the study of his word'? Psalm 53.3 uses, in a different context, the very same word that in the heading of Psalm 14 is used of a kind of psalm called the 'Maskil'. I've translated it 'song of understanding': in fact we've had a few of these already. In our worship and prayer and reading, we are called again and again to grow our understanding of God. Yes, it is a hard world: so we are continually challenged to pray, reflect and be open to God, even when – *especially* when – we seek the spirit of understanding in unexpected places.

*What are the biggest challenges in life, the ones that really do call for the biggest miracles?*

# WEEK 2

## It's an unjust world

# Monday

## No regrets?

———•◦•———

## Psalm 32

1 Of David. A song of understanding.
  Blessed is the one whose unjust actions are lifted off him and
  whose sins are made decent!
2 Blessed is the man whom the Lord does not hold guilty, and in
  whose spirit there is only honesty!
3 For while I kept it all hushed up, my very bones wore out in my
  roaring anguish all day long.
4 Because by day and by night your hand was heavy upon me,
  my strength waned as in the summer drought. *Selah.*
5 Then I declared my wrongdoing, I no longer covered up my
  guilt. I said, 'I will make confession for my sins to the Lord,'
  and you lifted the guilt of my sin off me. *Selah.*
6 And so, may each and every one of your faithful followers pray
  to you as soon as he realizes his own sins; only then will they
  not be caught up in the surging flood-waters!
7 You are a shelter for me, you guard me from distress; you
  encompass me with ringing cries of deliverance. *Selah.*
8 Let me give you understanding and teach you in the way that
  you are to go; let me offer you advice with my eye upon you.
9 Do not be like a horse or a mule: they have no intelligence;
  their steps have to be held in line by bit and bridle – may that
  not come near you!
10 There are many pains for the wrongdoer, but the one who
  trusts in the Lord, loving-kindness surrounds him.

<sup>11</sup> Be glad in the Lord and rejoice! Shout with joy, all you that are of upright heart!

Week 2 carries on our quest for understanding, with – as the heading tells us – another 'Maskil' psalm, as were Psalms 55 and 88 last week. Here, this fits with the first words of verses 1 and 2, a neat pair of verses (balanced pairs of phrases are typical in Hebrew poetry). 'Blessed is he who . . .' is a common formula in Hebrew wisdom poetry. We've seen it at the beginning of Psalms 1 and 119, rich as they are in teaching.

This very Jewish-teacher phrase might also remind you of the words of the Benedictus – 'Blessed is he who comes in the name of the Lord'. We hear it or say it if we go to Holy Communion. We consider it to be about Jesus: the rabbi well-versed in Jewish teaching.

Psalm 32 has much to teach those who pray it. It suggests we need to be honest with ourselves and with God about our shortcomings.

It gives the personal testimony of someone who has denied his own faults both to God and himself. The Psalmist tells his own story. There were things in his life he regretted. While he tried not to think of these flaws, avoiding them, his guilt truly weighed him down. When he honestly opened his mouth and was up-front with both God and himself, the burden was lifted and he was very glad. So he encourages others to learn from him and follow his example.

Learning from others' mistakes or examples helps us live better lives. 'Imitation is the highest form of flattery.' We try to be like those we look up to.

Here we have a holy person to look up to: a person who has learned his lesson and wants to help others learn it too. He was once a man who had things to regret. He tried to blot them out for himself, but that didn't work. Are there things that weigh on your conscience at the moment? Things you might have got wrong, or just not got right? The Psalmist says that trying to brush them under the carpet before God doesn't help. Rather, being honest about them, and offering them to God, will bring forgiveness, lightness of heart and joy.

Lent is a time for self-examination. Maybe you are well-nigh perfect. You don't drink, you don't smoke, you have excellent relationships with everyone around you, you recycle and have a simple lifestyle, you give a tenth of all you earn to charity, you go to church every Sunday and you pray every day. Nevertheless, as I hope you realize, something's still missing. Even the 'blessed' man at the beginning of Psalm 32 was not blessed because he was perfect in himself. He was blessed because he was honest about himself, and he knew his weaknesses and his need for continual forgiveness.

Are you honest with yourself? Honest about being small and mortal and limited? Honest about not being self-sufficient even when you're at the top of your game? Honest about all the things you have not being yours but being on loan to you? Honest about the times when you have lacked love for yourself, for other people, or for God?

Asking yourself that last question is one very traditional way to prepare for one-to-one Confession, or the individual Sacrament of Reconciliation – another name for the liturgy because it's about being reconciled with God personally, which in its broadest sense also involves being reconciled with others and with ourselves. It doesn't need to involve those wooden cubicles we see in churches across Europe, with one side for the priest and the other for the penitent. It is in fact also available for anyone in the Church of England if they want it, and it can happen in conversation with the vicar in a quiet pew in church or a front room at home, or with a priest at a retreat house. Some find that doing it formally can be very freeing. Drawing up three columns of notes, we can list the things we need to get off our chest, the times when we have lacked love for (1) God, (2) other people and (3) ourselves. This means of getting ready to make a formal Confession is modelled on Jesus' Great Love Commandment 'to love God . . . and to love your neighbour as yourself'. It's a good way of reflecting on life. Three people to love: God, neighbour and self.

Trying to get all this right is simply impossible. Sometimes it seems as if we have to choose between God and our neighbour, our neighbour and ourselves, or God and ourselves. Do we hurry to get up to go to church, or do we stay in bed and get a bit more rest once in a while? Do we rush past the homeless person in the street on our way to the evening service, or do we stop and chat and buy him a coffee – and be late to church? Do we tell a friend we simply can't do something, because we know we need to look after ourselves, perhaps just for once? Our daily dilemmas may only be tiny, but each one highlights this fact – we can't do it all by ourselves.

It's this 'I can't do it all by myself' that expresses the true, honest humility that comes in self-examination and confession. We may think that 'Confession' as we've just explored it is a traditional or high church thing to do, and not for us. But nearly *every service* in church has a certain amount of confession in it. That may come in the form of the 'General Confession', where everyone says together some words about having sinned, followed by a prayer about forgiveness. Or it may simply come as that line in the Lord's Prayer, 'Forgive us our sins as we forgive those who sin against us' (or the traditional version, using 'trespass' instead of 'sin').

Even if we're making a pretty good effort at life, every day we all need to recognize that we can never do it by ourselves. Our lives are totally dependent on God. As soon as we realize that, it will give us true lightness of spirit, and a very grounded reason for rejoicing.

*What weighs on your heart?*

# Tuesday

## It makes me angry

———◆◆◆———

## Psalm 137

1    By the rivers of Babylon, there we sat down, oh, and we wept,
     when we remembered Zion,
2    on the poplars there we hung our lyres,
3    because it was there that our captors asked us for a song, and
     our tormentors asked us for mirth: 'Sing to us one of the songs
     of Zion!'
4    How could we sing a song of the LORD on foreign soil?
5    If I forget you, O Jerusalem, let my right hand wither away!
6    Let my tongue stick to the roof of my mouth if I do not
     remember you, and if I do not put Jerusalem first above my
     highest joy!
7    Remember, O LORD, against the Edomites, the day Jerusalem
     fell! They said, 'Lay it bare, lay it bare, even to its foundations!'
8    Daughter Babylon, you are undone! Blessed is the one who
     pays you back for the dealings you have dealt us!
9    Blessed is he who snatches and smashes to pieces your children
     against the cliff face!

This horrifically chilling psalm makes us wonder how such violence
and hatred can really be included in a book we thought was all about
worship. Aren't the Psalms supposedly spiritual songs, hymns, carefully put-together words to be used in the church or synagogue?
How on earth can we be content to sing, or even read, such dreadful
words as those in the final two verses?

Some churches don't. They simply leave them out, along with many other verses in the Psalms that are vicious, violent, vitriolic. Had Christ edited the Psalter before it was handed down to us, wouldn't he have cut them out? After all, didn't he tell us to love our enemies? Isn't that what we were saying in the context of Psalm 53 just last Saturday?

Jesus didn't take a year out to make the Hebrew Scriptures say just what we think he might want them to say. I suspect he'd have vehemently refused to do that. After all, he says that 'until heaven and earth pass away, not one letter, not even a part of a letter, will pass away from the law until all is accomplished' (Matthew 5.18). He values every letter of the Scriptures. This would have included the psalms that he sang and knew back to front.

There's no evidence that anyone even in the centuries during which the Psalter was formed would have chosen to slice out the unsavoury bits. There's no collection of manuscripts remotely like that (unless we haven't found it yet). So we just have to try and make sense of all the verses that we find most difficult. That applies throughout the Bible, not just in the Old Testament.

The first three verses of Psalm 137 project a picture of great pathos. Echoing the trauma of Psalm 74, Psalm 137 immediately draws us into the tragedy of the fall of Jerusalem. Verses 4–6 are a psychological exploration of what the people of Jerusalem now in exile in Babylon are going through. They want to remember Jerusalem, but how? They don't want to give their captors the pleasure of even a single song. Yet remember Jerusalem they absolutely must, for their own sense of identity; life would be meaningless without the city which has shaped them and their beliefs. Jerusalem is in all seriousness the most profound joy-giving thought: the 'highest joy' of verse 6 is the same word, 'mirth', used facetiously by the Babylonians in verse 3. The Babylonians will get what they asked for: a song of Zion.

What more appropriate, then, than a lament? The moment the exiles start remembering Jerusalem, they begin conjuring up memories for themselves of a Jerusalem that was last seen smouldering in ruins. Now, they hear not the present taunts of their captors, which are tame by comparison: rather, they hear the shouts of their enemies urging one another on in bringing about the utter destruction of

Jerusalem. The words that are used shudder with the language of sexual as well as military assault: cities were referred to in feminine forms. 'Daughter Babylon' here echoes the implied 'daughter Zion', a Hebrew phrase used to describe Jerusalem. The attackers' challenge is to raze the city to the ground, literally to 'lay her bare'. The shouts echo once again in the ears of the exiles.

It's then that those blood-curdling verses come in to close the psalm. There's plenty of reason to get angry, the sense of injustice has quickly bubbled over. This anger now turns against the captors who are teasing the exiles. That request for a song has backfired: invoking memories of Jerusalem has turned these lyre players into people capable of killing children with their bare hands. Even more terrifying is the repeated 'Blessed is he' formula which, as in Psalm 32, is more commonly a sign of wisdom or understanding.

The Babylonians have unleashed a fury that bites back. Against their captors, the helpless exiles have only one defence: those very songs the Babylonians have requested. The exiles can still call upon their God, the God of Jerusalem. They cry to God in just the way they have learnt, through years of worship in the Temple. This is an honest and heartfelt cry to God for help, a wail that holds nothing back. It looks to God to avenge their suffering, even their bereavements of their own children. The surrounded exiles can only imagine being in the position to grab their enemies' children and destroy the future generation. Their 'blessing' is in fact a curse, but it's a hostile action that they rely above all on God to carry out.

It's still hard to swallow that our God might be capable of such an atrocity, even when his people have been so angered by what they have gone through. We need a God of justice, yes. But we also need a God who is big enough to hear and receive all our prayers, our very selves. What I take from this psalm above all else is the invitation to throw our most unpleasant, most angry, most damaged and damaging prayers and thoughts at God. Life can sometimes make us angry, and more. But God wants us to give that anger to him, just as much as he wants our sweetness and light. We need to hand over our unfinished business, our desperation and frustration to him. We are to entrust our whole selves, our whole lives – however unsavoury – to him.

After all, God is a God who, in Jesus, knew the bloody messiness of human life all too well.

*Do you have angry thoughts or feelings you can hand over to God?*

# Wednesday

## Only God can judge

———•◦•———

## Psalm 50

1  A psalm of Asaph. God, the Creator God, the Lord, spoke: he has called the earth from the place where the sun rises in the east to the place where it sets.

2  Out of Zion, the perfection of beauty, the Creator God shines forth.

3  Let our God come! and let him not be silent! An all-consuming fire goes before him, and it storms fiercely around him.

4  He calls to the heavens above, and to the earth, for the trial of his people:

5  'Gather to me my devoted ones, who made a covenant with me over sacrifice!'

6  Then the heavens declared his righteousness, for God is judge. *Selah.*

7  'Hear this, my people, and let me speak, O Israel, and let me testify against you. I am God, your God.

8  It's not because of your sacrifices that I rebuke you, not for your burnt-offerings which are continually before me.

9  I claim no young bull from your households, from your enclosures no goats:

10  for to me belongs every wild beast in the forest, the cattle on a thousand hills;

11  I know every bird of the mountains, and all that moves in the fields is mine.

12  If I were hungry, I would not tell you! because to me belongs the world and all that fills it.

13  Do I really eat the flesh of bulls, or drink the blood of goats?
14  Sacrifice to God a thanksgiving, and obey your vows to the
    Most High God.
15  Call to me in the day of your trouble: I shall deliver you and
    you shall honour me!'
16  But, to the wicked, this is what God says:
    'What is it to you to tell of my statutes, or to raise my covenant
    to your lips?
17  For you hate discipline, and you push my words behind you!
18  If you see a thief, you are pleased to be with him; and you
    have your place among adulterers!
19  You use your mouth for evil, and your tongue spins deceit!
20  You sit and speak against your brother, to your own mother's
    son you account fault.
21  All this you have done, and I kept silent; so now you think I am
    like you . . .
    Let me reproach you, let me set it all out before your very eyes:
22  You need to understand this, you who forget God, so that I
    don't tear you apart with no one to help you!
23  The one who sacrifices thanksgiving, he is the one who truly
    honours me; the one who sets his way straight, I shall reveal to
    him the salvation of God.'

This intriguing psalm describes a heavenly law suit. God has set up a court to judge his people. It's a strongly worded way of trying to set them straight – but notice that for all the threats, everyone seems to be given a second chance in the light of what they have learned at this trial.

After the heading (Psalms 73–83 are also attributed to Asaph), God is introduced. This psalm is all about God, not about the Psalmist or mankind. God is speaking. Maybe this is more prophecy than prayer. This is God teaching his people, communicating with them, correcting them and trying to set them straight. The Psalmist tried to instruct us; now God educates us about himself directly.

What's more, God is referred to at the outset by three names: El, Elohim and Yahweh. Back on Ash Wednesday we heard the name YHWH, the covenant name of God, revealed at the burning bush. El and Elohim both mean 'God' more generically; 'Elohim' is a plural form, or 'royal we'. The words 'El' and 'Elohim' were used by other people rather than the Israelites. When the Israelites used them along with 'Yahweh' to name the same God, they did so to claim that God was the 'God of gods'; that he was the most important of all the ancient Near Eastern gods of neighbouring peoples; and that this was the true God that everyone had been looking up to all their lives.

In the first couple of verses here I've rendered Elohim 'Creator God': it's the first name of God used in the Bible, and is employed throughout the creation stories at the beginning of Genesis. This is the name that's used throughout most of this psalm. It's the one Lord, the only Lord, who convenes his court, but he has a range of different names, just as Jesus has lots of different names – Christ, Messiah, Saviour, and so on. When we love people, we might use different names for them: not just their Christian names, but other names which are special to us and our particular relationships.

God is both judge and accuser here. The skies and the earth – the whole universe – are his witnesses to the actions of mankind. There's nothing at all that God is not in relationship with, there's no secret that we can hide from him. God is judge of all, because he knows everything, he 'knows all the secrets of our hearts' (as in the marriage service). Then God turns to the accused: mankind.

God addresses two kinds of people. First there are those who carry out the rituals but whose hearts aren't in it. Second there are those who simply don't try; they're more likely to be found in the company of petty criminals or those who don't really care. Both these groups of people are told to buck their ideas up. Yet it's interesting that there's no sign of the perfect people here – even God's *hasidim* (verse 5), the ones who have a share in his loving-kindness, his covenant people, have to do better. It's uncomfortable to think that there are only two kinds of people in the world: those who try to be good but don't succeed; and those who don't even try to be good.

God has lowered the bar. He does not need empty rituals from those who are trying to live up to being his people; you don't have to go off and make luscious sacrifices. 'What good does that do?' he asks. 'Think about it – do I really need bulls and choice offerings? No, of course not; what I want above all is your thanksgiving,' he says in verse 14.

This is a great verse. Remember that the Eucharist is literally 'the thanksgiving'. It too has many different titles – the Lord's Supper, the Mass, Communion – but above all, it is Thanksgiving. Christians can bring a particular layer of interpretation to this verse. Join in both 'thanksgiving' to God, and 'the Thanksgiving' to God. That's something that on every level we can offer to God without ceasing, whether in church, or at home, or just going about our daily business.

And 'obey your vows to the Most High God'? There's yet another name for God, one again based on the 'El' name. Many of us will have taken baptismal vows, or confirmation vows, or wedding vows, and some of us reading this book together will even have taken vows to the religious life, or ordination vows. Brothers and sisters reading together, we may not know one another, but we are all called to the Christian faith, and we are all called to vows in living out that life. Being 'devoted' is literally about having made vows. We are all called to consecrate ourselves to God.

Vows demand obedience, and that helps us in our godly living. Monks, nuns, friars and sisters – the 'Religious' – will have made vows of one sort or another to obedience. If obedience helps us to live up to our God-given calling, then surely we want to obey all the time? Discipline can be truly joyful. If only we could be better at it!

Above all we are called to sincerity in our 'devotions'. To do our best to make sure that our hearts are in it, that our minds aren't wandering, and neither are our footsteps. What vows do you need to uphold today and every day?

*Does the idea of God as judge of all challenge or comfort you?*

# Thursday

## *Just confession*

———•◆•———

### Psalm 51

1  To the Director of Music: A psalm of David –
2  when Nathan the Prophet went to him about David's going in to Bathsheba.
3  Have mercy on me, O God, because of your loving-kindness; because of your great compassion blot out my wrongdoing!
4  Again and again wash out from me my guilt, and from my sin cleanse me!
5  For my transgressions, yes, I do know them; and my sins are ever at the front of my mind.
6  Against you, you especially, I have sinned, and I have done evil in your sight. Therefore you are just in your sentence and entirely right in your judgement.
7  Indeed, with guilt was I born, and in sin my mother conceived me.
8  Indeed, sincerity deep down is what gives you delight, and deep in my soul wisdom is what you teach me.
9  Purify me with hyssop so that I may be clean; wash me so that you might make me whiter than snow!
10  Make it so that I hear joy and gladness, let the bones you have crushed rejoice!
11  Hide your face from my sins and wipe away all my iniquities.
12  Create in me a clean heart, O God, and make my spirit within me be newly steady.
13  Do not cast me away from your presence, and do not take your Holy Spirit from me.

14 Make the joy of your salvation come back to me, and a generous spirit – please sustain me!

15 So may I teach sinners your ways, that those who have gone astray will return to you.

16 Save me from guilt of shedding blood, O God, God of my rescue, that my tongue will shout with joy because of your righteousness!

17 O Lord, open my lips, and let my mouth declare your praise.

18 For you do not delight in sacrifice, or I would give that to you, and a burnt-offering does not please you.

19 Sacrifices that please God are a humble spirit, a humble and contrite heart: that, O God, you will not despise.

20 Prosper Zion with your goodwill, build up the walls of Jerusalem.

21 Then you will accept sacrifices offered in righteousness, burnt-offerings and whole-offerings; then bulls will be offered on your altar.

Back on Ash Wednesday we thought about David, and how Psalm 51 is supposed to be linked with David's act of having Uriah the Hittite killed so David could take Uriah's wife Bathsheba for himself (verse 2).

Morally corrupt, David was nevertheless considered exemplary in penitence. This was a long-held tradition: verse 2 with its reference to Bathsheba seems to have been added at the time of the exile. This couldn't actually have all taken place in David's time, because in the last two lines of the psalm Jerusalem is in ruins, whereas it wasn't when David was king. Rather, the Jews in exile probably adapted this psalm, connecting David's repentance with their own penitential setting. If the exile was a punishment, then the exiles thought they must have much to repent. Who would be a better teacher of repentance than David, king and Psalmist?

There are words about cleansing, washing, purifying, making white again, like Lady Macbeth's frantic scrubbing away of an illusory bloodstain: 'Out, damned spot!' The penitent in Psalm 51 is so profoundly remorseful that we might think he's trying to wash away the worst of sins, murder. (Certainly in verse 16 he prays that he might be saved from blood-guilt, but that could be because either he does have blood on his hands, or he fears being an even worse sinner than he thinks he is already.)

Verse upon verse is heaped up: devout prayers for mercy in verses 3–4 are balanced by real acknowledgement of sinfulness. This humility could not really go any lower: it traces guilt back not only to birth, but even to the conception of the embryo. God is entirely in the right, the Psalmist in the wrong. It's as if God has accused him – just as in the previous psalm. This seems like a personal response to yesterday's divine trial in Psalm 50.

Washing, cleansing – these are also symbolized in baptism, and the vows we take at that time. The water of baptism is a sign of dying to sin and rising to new life: water gives life, and water cleanses and purifies. We use water to help us remember our baptism, dipping a finger in a water-stoup at the church door, or in the font, signing ourselves with the cross. It's a physical reminder that we have turned away from sin and to Christ, we've been washed clean by the blood of Christ.

All this comes centuries after Psalm 51 was written. But the symbolism was already there. No surprise it was taken up by John the Baptist in the desert as he prepared for the coming of Christ, his powerful acts of baptism in the River Jordan signifying repentance from sins. Like Lady Macbeth, we can wash outward dirt away, but we can't wash away inward filth. We need more than water for that. We need God's Holy Spirit.

It's inward transformation we desire. Renew a right spirit within me, says the Psalmist. He knows he needs God way more than a good bath. God wants not just an outward show of piety but a truly transformational one. God wants heartfelt humility. *That* is a sacrifice God will not despise.

That's transformational because it gives profound stability in life (verse 12). Acknowledging honestly that we need God, that we have deeply ingrained flaws which we can't deal with by ourselves, that we have weaknesses or past hurts which make us vulnerable in turn to hurting others: this takes us back to our very roots. It brings us down to the ground. Humility is absolutely where humanity needs to be: we are creatures of the 'humus', or soil, creatures who are earthy, grounded. We are to recognize our lowliness, our smallness and our dependence on God. We need God to make up for us where our love is lacking. As Christians, especially thinking about it at this time of year, we believe Jesus' Passion, death and resurrection most centrally show how God can make up even the direst lack of love humanity can manage.

But it's also very hard to weigh up our sin. If we confess again and again, and are too hard on ourselves about our past wrongdoing, we risk lacking love towards ourselves. We also risk gaining a false kind of self-deprecating humility, a humility that actually becomes a sort of pride. It's in danger of becoming an eternal circle. What God in Jesus comes to do is break that circle. It's the same in this psalm too. True confession is accepted by God. The forgiven sinner is freed to rejoice in God's salvation (verses 16–17).

Maybe this psalm – or at least part of it – does go back to the exile. Sometimes when life collapses around us, as Jerusalem collapsed around the exiles, we think we're to blame. It's a natural reaction, but it's probably not the whole story. What we can take from Psalm 51 is that as long as we weigh up carefully, profoundly, honestly what deep down we most need to confess – the 'spot' that is always on our minds – God will, by his grace, build us up from the most earthy and stable foundations possible.

*How does forgiveness change you?*

# *Friday*

## *On the verge of injustice*

-------••••-------

## Psalm 22

¹ To the Director of Music: according to the tune 'Dawn Doe'.
A psalm of David.

² My God, my God, why have you forsaken me? Why are you so
far from saving me, and from my anguished roaring?

³ My God, I cry to you by day, and you do not answer; and by
night, and there is no peace for me!

⁴ But you are the Holy One, you are enthroned, the praise of Israel.

⁵ In you our fathers trusted; they trusted and you brought them
to safety.

⁶ To you they cried and they were saved; in you they trusted and
were not disappointed.

⁷ But I am a worm, and not a man, scorned by men and
despised by people.

⁸ All those who see me deride me; they pull faces, they shake
their heads.

⁹ 'Throw yourself on the LORD! Let him deliver him, let him save
him, for he's the one who delights in him!'

¹⁰ Yes, it was you who drew me out of the womb, you who made
me trusting on my mother's breasts.

¹¹ On you was I cast from birth, from my mother's womb you
have been my God.

¹² Do not be far from me, because trouble is near and because
there is no one to help.

¹³ They surround me, bulls, many of them, mighty bulls of
Bashan encircle me.

14 They open their mouths over me; they are lions, with tearing teeth, and roaring.

15 Like the waters am I poured out, and my bones are dislocated; my heart has become like wax melting deep within me.

16 My strength dries up like fired clay, and my tongue sticks on the roof of my mouth, and I am set in the dust of death.

17 For they surround me, dogs, a gang of them, evil ones; they are all around me like lions setting on my hands and my feet.

18 I count all my bones, and they gaze at me, they look me over.

19 They divide up my clothes between themselves, over my garment they throw lots.

20 But you, O Lord, do not be far away, oh my God, hurry to help me!

21 Deliver my life from the sword, my one and only life from the clutches of the dog!

22 Save me from the lion's mouth, and from the horns of the wild ox. You have answered me!

23 Let me tell of your name to my brothers, in the heart of the great congregation let me praise you!

24 You who fear the Lord, praise him! All you of the family of Jacob, honour him! Stand in awe of him, all you of the family of Israel!

25 For he did not despise, he did not detest the afflictions of the humble man; he did not hide his face from him; when he cried for help to him, he listened.

26 Because of you I give praise in the great congregation, my vows will I fulfil in the sight of those who fear God.

27 Let them eat, the poor, and let them be filled. Let them praise the Lord, those who seek him. May your hearts live for ever!

28 Let them remember and turn back to the Lord, all the ends of the earth, and let them bow down before you, all the families of the peoples.

29 For true kingship is the Lord's, and he rules over the nations.

30 Practically already have they eaten and prostrated themselves, all the rich ones of the earth! all those going down into the dust, those whose souls are barely alive, shall bow down to him.

³¹   The next generation shall serve him, and all about the Lord will be told again to the generation after.

³²   They shall come and shall tell of his righteousness to people yet to be born, for he has acted.

Yesterday we read the psalm associated with Ash Wednesday. Psalm 22 is connected to Good Friday. There's a lot here that apparently looks forward to Jesus' Passion and crucifixion, even though Jesus came after the Psalms were composed and collected together. Let's explore some of these moments.

Verse 2 is what Jesus says on the cross according to the Gospels of Matthew and Mark. It's hard to think of Jesus accusing God, his Father, of forsaking him – especially since these are Jesus' last words. How can the Son of God be forsaken by God? Maybe he wasn't: maybe even Jesus' own faith had been so tried and tested that it was now shattered . . . But in that case, how can we get our heads around the idea that Jesus apparently lost his faith during the most extreme suffering?

We can't know what Jesus was feeling or thinking, but it's quite believable that Jesus said these words on the cross because he knew the Psalms so well. When you need to pray and you're in dire circumstances, you come out with age-old words and rhythms from your earliest prayers, the simplest things you've learned about God. Jesus the Rabbi taught people how to pray. It wouldn't surprise us to hear the Lord's Prayer on a dying Christian's lips today; it needn't trouble us that the dying Jesus thought of a common lament, an early verse from a psalm. It tells us that in dire pain, Jesus called upon his Scriptures. His prayer habits are right there for us all to see: a Jewish faith which meant that even feeling deeply forsaken and utterly alone he could still cry out to God. In these two Gospels, the Psalms were his last word.

What's rather more astonishing is that the bystanders didn't realize it. That's probably because Jesus was praying in Aramaic (effectively the widespread spoken dialect of Hebrew at the time), which wasn't quite the pure Hebrew of the 'official', canonical, version of Psalm 22. Jesus really had made these ancient texts his own.

Verse 7 forms an aria in Handel's *Messiah*, 'He was despised'. We've grown used to thinking about references to Jesus in the Old

Testament, because there are layers of Christian tradition which interpret the Hebrew Scriptures in the light of the New Testament. Jesus sometimes used Old Testament prophecies to refer to himself, or to explain his dying and resurrection; Christians ever since have done so too, in music, art and literature. But of course the Psalmist didn't have Jesus in mind when he composed this psalm. Jesus and his Passion and resurrection were still in the future. The psalm more generally therefore reflects a sadly all-too-common human experience of being threatened, being on the verge of great, undeserved harm.

Psalm 22 reminds us that unfair trials, fickle mob rule, undeserved blame and punishment can happen to anyone. Jesus' story is not that he's the only one who's treated unjustly. Rather, he is joining the throngs of others who suffer injustice. He comes alongside the many oppressed, poor, bullied, wronged people in our world. It's simply most obviously unjust when Love Incarnate gets the blame for everything that was wrong in first-century Jerusalem and Judaea.

There are some remarkable coincidences between this ancient psalm and the Gospel stories. Verses 13–16 and the vicious wild beasts setting upon the Psalmist quickly conjure up images for us of Jesus being surrounded and beaten by Roman soldiers. One translation of verse 17, informed by a Christian tradition, reads 'they pierce my hands and feet', but it's tricky to get this from the Hebrew, and it's not actually cited in any of the Gospels.

Verse 18 *is* quoted, though, remarkably, in all four Gospels. The four Evangelists clearly understood Jesus' crucifixion in the light of Psalm 22, regardless of whether Jesus himself did. Reordering the verses of the psalm, a few verses later in Matthew's account are separate quotations from verses 8–9; Mark too depicts onlookers deriding Jesus in words recalling verse 8, but with different words of mockery.

Did the Evangelists see Jesus as a fulfilment of Psalm 22? Yes. Did Jesus see himself as a fulfilment of Psalm 22? Probably no more than anyone in dreadful suffering. And in verse 21 there's the clear sense that this life is it, there's nothing afterwards; Jesus however clearly proclaimed otherwise. So although Matthew and Mark attribute the quotation of verse 2 to Jesus on the cross, I suspect that Jesus wouldn't have seen himself as the one and only enactment of this psalm.

After all, Psalm 22 is not about a specific situation or person. It's there to stand for the dreadful injustices so many suffer. When the Gospels use it to talk about Jesus, they are actually conveying the messages that we can see Jesus prefigured in the Hebrew Scriptures; that Jesus knew the Hebrew Bible thoroughly; and that Jesus joined the suffering of 'everyman'. Because he joined humanity in this worldwide, age-old cycle of pain and injustice, so we hope we can join him and journey together towards God.

Let's not forget the happy ending. In verse 22, God has answered this prayer. There is salvation and praise. There is continuing teaching for generations to come of God's power and goodness. So confident is the Psalmist of this joyous outcome that in verse 30 it's as if the future celebrations have already happened. Now *that's* more Jesus' style.

*What injustices do you flee?*

# Saturday
## Just rule

---

## Psalm 82

1    A psalm of Asaph.
     God stands in the assembly of gods, among them he gives
     judgement.
2    'How long will you judge unjustly and favour the wicked?'
     *Selah.*
3    Give justice to the bottom-class man and to the orphan, give
     righteousness to the troubled and the poor,
4    Save the dregs of society and the very needy ones: save them
     all from the hand of criminals!'
5    They do not know, they just don't get it, they wander around
     in darkness; they are shaken, even the foundations of the
     earth.
6    I had said, 'You are gods, sons of the Most High, all of you' –
7    But surely like mankind you shall die, like any other leader you
     shall fall.
8    Arise, O God, judge the earth, for to you do all the nations
     belong!

Thank God not every trial is like Jesus' trial! We want justice, we
want to be able to trust lawyers and legal systems. We want fairness.
After all, it's what young children commonly cry: 'It's not fair!'

Life sometimes isn't fair. We want God to put it right. That is the
hope and prayer and picture of Psalm 82.

This psalm pictures a divine law court, as does Psalm 50. Except
this time it's just God who is the judge. This is our God. He is imagined with other gods gathered around him. But unlike the heavens

and the earth of Psalm 50, who are witnesses, this get-together of gods is in fact the dock. They are the ones who stand accused.

Psalm 50 showed God accusing mankind. The book of Job shows mankind accusing God. Psalm 82 shows God accusing other gods.

Isn't that odd? Isn't there only one God?

Psalm 50 was probably influenced by the ancient Near Eastern myths of peoples and nations bordering Israel, polytheistic lands and tribes who worshipped many gods. Israel can claim to have the 'best' God, because he is the most just God. He's the one who speaks out in their council, he's in the place to judge them. Society sometimes talks about 'alpha males'; this is like 'alpha God'. God is the leader of them all, the big chief – all because he is both judge and justice.

What kind of justice is this? In verses 3–4, God speaks out to support the poorest, most overlooked people in society. Now Israelite culture wasn't the kind of class-based society we know today. Picture a family where children are at risk of being taken into care because of neglect; foster children being shunted around from house to house; addicts troubled by their substance abuse and the mental health problems it has caused; those suffering psychological disturbances, and whose troubles no one quite knows how to ease; those who can't afford either to keep their homes warm (if they have a home), or even to buy the reduced-price leftovers from the supermarket at the end of the day. It's the most vulnerable in our society – or even outside our society, because they're frequently hidden not just under the surface, but beyond the edges of our vision – who are most at risk of being preyed upon in rough company, by drugs barons, thieves, pimps and so on. It is these God is calling to mind as he rebukes the other gods – for someone must have let this injustice happen. God puts these people at the top of the priority list for justice. This is a revolutionary society about to break forth.

In a welfare state, we can too easily think, 'Ah well, these are other people's problems. There are psychiatric nurses in the community who look after people like that. Social services. GPs. In the worst scenarios, perhaps the police . . .' It's telling that while 'orphan' is a word often used in the Psalms to refer to children, it's not one Western societies are often likely to apply these days to anyone under 18. Any youngster so unfortunate is described rather as being 'in care'.

National health institutions, care packages, specialist bodies set up by local authorities, lull us into the mindset that the poor and needy aren't our responsibility, but the State's.

But they *are* our responsibility; and God in Psalm 82 claims the very highest responsibility for them. He provides them with imagined legal aid, tends to their needs, and dismisses the other judges who formerly claimed authority. These 'gods' don't get it, says our God (verse 5). They just don't get their responsibility and what that means. In fact, they're so irresponsible about this, they should no longer be regarded as 'gods, sons of the Most High' (verse 6).

Watching God's judgement of those who have failed to live up to the mark in delivering justice, we might again think, 'That's for *them* to worry about.' But let's not miss the mark ourselves. After all, these failed 'gods' are then likened to human leaders (verse 7). Both human leaders and failed gods will fall and die. Only our God stands way above all this.

Hang on a moment. Does this mean that we too are challenged to avoid being like these failed so-called gods? Absolutely. For doesn't Jesus invite us to become part of his family, his brothers and sisters, and therefore sons and daughters of God, 'sons of the Most High'? So we all have a responsibility to our community, to our world. We can't just sit back and let God be the only one fighting for justice. We have to add our own voice to the struggle. That's what God's just rule is really about: enfranchising all the nations – for all belong to God – to share in a just society.

That might mean volunteering in a local advice bureau or charity shop. It might mean helping out in a soup kitchen, or even simply stopping and giving a homeless person not only a meal deal from the nearest shop, but also some conversation. It might mean lobbying our politicians about climate change and the risks it poses to the poorest in our world.

Psalm 82 says that the thing that makes God most God-like is justice. God the just judge answers the basic cry of humanity: 'It's not fair!' It may be an unjust world, but we can engage with God's just rule, by praying and playing our part in bringing justice to all the families of the nations.

*What might a just world look like?*

# WEEK 3

## It's a big world

# Monday

## *Faith beyond boundaries*

---

### Psalm 2

1   Why are nations in tumult, and peoples murmuring emptinesses?

2   They take powerful stances, the kings of the earth, and those who rule sit in parliament together against the Lord and against the one he has anointed:

3   'Let us rip apart their iron bonds, and cast away from us their twisted cords!'

4   The one who sits in heaven – he laughs! The Lord – he is derisive to them!

5   And then, he will speak to them in his fury, and in his burning anger he will terrify them:

6   'I have installed my king on Zion, my holy hill.'

7   Let me recount the command of the Lord. He said to me, 'My son, that's who you are; I have this day given you birth.

8   Ask of me, that I may give the nations as your inheritance, and the ends of the earth as your heirloom.

9   You will break them with a rod of iron, and like a china teacup you will smash them to pieces.'

10   Now therefore, O kings, have this insight; be chastened, you who judge the earth:

11   serve the Lord in fear, and be excited to the point of trembling!

12   Kiss his son, or he will be angry, and your way perish; for his anger burns in a few moments. Blessed are all those who seek their protection in him.

In Psalm 82, God compared unjust and failed 'gods' to human leaders. There's a similar faultline here between God and God's anointed, and the 'kings of the earth' – 'those who rule' who are sitting 'in parliament together' against God and his anointed king (verse 2).

Let's start with God and the godly human leader, the king in Jerusalem. (This would have been well after King David's time.) A king was anointed, with a ceremony of installation, at which he was set in place. Anointing was very common in the ancient Near East. Kings like David were anointed, in his case when he was young, picked out among Jesse's sons for leadership in the years to come (1 Samuel 16). Anointing was also carried out for healing, because of the soothing and health-giving qualities of olive oil, a common commodity in Israel. The Church today still anoints for healing, and uses oils at baptism, confirmation and ordination. Anointing has also been the most holy part of the consecration service of an English monarch through the centuries. It remains a powerful symbol.

And so it should, for 'Christ' in Greek literally means 'the anointed one'. That's also what 'Messiah' means, in the Hebrew and Aramaic languages. In the Gospels of Matthew and Mark, Peter is the first one to call Jesus 'the Christ', in a pivotal conversation at Caesarea Philippi (Matthew 16; Mark 8). Jesus is also anointed shortly before he dies, and he uses this striking gesture to forewarn of his coming death. More traditionally, according to Jewish custom, the women go to the tomb intending to anoint him after his death (Mark 16). It is with their oils and spices in their hands that they hear the astonishing news of his resurrection.

The anointed one in Psalm 2 is referred to as 'son of God'. To us, it's odd that God can say he has 'given birth' to his son today. But the ancient Near Eastern language of adoption powerfully links God with his anointed. On the day he was anointed, the king became not just king but 'son of God', acknowledging the king's closeness to the divine. The king was essentially set apart, in a special place, and enthroned right next to God.

Geographically speaking, the king's palace was right alongside the Temple on Mount Zion (now called the Temple Mount). This was the very hub of Jerusalem, its spiritual, judicial and symbolic beating heart. Zion, the holy hill, was not only the place of the Temple and the royal palace, but it also stood for the whole of Jerusalem. A number of psalms focus on this so-called 'Zion theology'; Psalm 2 introduces this early on, in the edition of the Psalms which has been passed down to us today.

The contrast between God and God's anointed on the one hand, and the kings of the earth on the other, is just like the contrast between Zion on the one hand, and the nations and the ends of the earth on the other. God breaks boundaries by making all the nations, not just Zion, the king's inheritance (verses 8–9). At the same time, he breaks boundaries by making all the peoples bow down to Zion's king rather than their own (verses 10–12).

These other leaders apparently thought they were great. They are described as getting together and flexing their muscles. This makes God laugh (verse 4)! Their strength was as nothing to God's. And then God gets really angry (verse 5). You don't want to make God angry, says the Psalmist: it's not pleasant (verse 9). So just get over yourselves, get down on your knees, all those in power, and look up to *my* King (verses 10–12). Can you imagine all the nations of the world, in the different video clips we see on the news, being obedient to one king? Especially to a totally uncorrupt one, who won't be persuaded to treat one or two insiders better than others? Mind-boggling.

Ours is a big world. There's much we will never know about it, many countries and peoples we will never encounter. And we're talking about absolutely the whole world here. Although the Psalmist could only have had awareness of neighbouring peoples, his reference to the entire world as he knew it is as good as saying simply 'the whole world'.

Now that too seems odd: hadn't God chosen the Israelites as his one and only people? And now he wants all people to act like his people?

There are other parts of the Hebrew Bible that hint at a similarly universal message. Isaiah 40—55 considers the whole world as part of God's saving plan. Jesus was into breaking boundaries, connecting not just with the Jewish people but also with those on the margins. He talked about and spent time with Samaritans, for instance – and they were generally shunned as Jews who had gone off the rails, so they were worse than anyone in the eyes of most first-century Jews. In due course, the Acts of the Apostles would develop the gospel into a message of hope for many different peoples and languages and cultures. That's the work we do as the Church continues today. To us a message of universalism isn't surprising; but it would have been for many ancient readers.

The psalm's closing words are 'Blessed are all those who seek their protection in him.' Using the 'Blessed is . . .' formula in Psalms 1 and 2, it's as if the Psalmist is saying, 'Now that's what I call wisdom.' It's a great way to launch into the rest of the Psalter.

*What boundaries do you think of Jesus crossing?*

# Tuesday

*From the sea . . .*

———————

## Psalm 107.1–32, 43

1    Praise the Lord, because he is good, because his loving-kindness is for ever! –

2    thus let the redeemed of the Lord say, those whom he redeemed from the hand of the enemy,

3    Those whom he gathered together from the lands, from the east and the west, from the north and the sea.

4    Some, in the desert, in the wilderness, that's where they were when they lost their way; they did not find a city to settle in;

5    hungry and thirsty, their spirit fell faint.

6    *Then they cried out to the Lord in their distress, and he delivered them from all their troubles.*

7    And he led them by a straight path to get to a city where they could settle.

8    *Let them praise the Lord for his loving-kindness, and for his awesome works for humanity's generations!*

9    For he has satisfied the thirsty, and the hungry soul he fills with good things.

10   Some, in deep shadowy darkness, that's where they were when they sat as prisoners of affliction and iron chains.

11   Because they rebelled against the words of God and they spurned the counsel of the Most High,

12   so he humbled their hearts through suffering, they fell and there was no one to help.

13   *Then they cried out to the Lord in their distress, and he saved them from all their troubles.*

14  He brought them out from the deep shadowy darkness, and he tore apart their shackles.

15  *Let them praise the LORD for his loving-kindness, and for his awesome works for humanity's generations!*

16  For he shattered the doors of bronze, and he cut through the bars of iron.

17  Some there were who were foolish in the way of their sinfulness, and for their unfair dealings they suffered:

18  all food was abhorrent to them, and they reached the gates of death.

19  *Then they cried out to the LORD in their distress, and he saved them from all their troubles.*

20  He sent his word and he healed them, and rescued them from their pits.

21  *Let them praise the LORD for his loving-kindness, and for his awesome works for humanity's generations!*

22  Let them offer thanksgiving sacrifices, and tell out what he has done in joyful song.

23  Some, in ships on the sea, that's where they were, where they went out plying their trade on mighty waters.

24  Now these ones, they really have seen the deeds of the LORD, and *his awesome works* in deep water.

25  He spoke and raised up a stormy wind which made the waves surge.

26  One minute they were going up to the heavens, the next they were heading down to the depths – their spirit melted away in their trouble.

27  They reeled and tottered like a drunk, and all their wisdom was swallowed up.

28  *Then they cried out to the LORD in their distress, and he* brought *them* out of *all their troubles.*

29  He stopped the storm to a whisper, and the waves were silent.

30  They rejoiced because the waves were quiet, and he steered them into the port they desired.

31  *Let them praise the LORD for his loving-kindness, and for his awesome works for humanity's generations!*

³²  So let them exalt him in the assembly of the people, and in the council of the elders let them praise him!

⁴³  Whoever is wise, let him store up all this and let him understand the loving-kindness of the Lᴏʀᴅ!

It's a big world, says the Psalmist: people everywhere are called to look to God. From all corners – from east and west, north and south (or 'the sea', as the Psalmist says, introducing an important theme in this psalm) – God redeems people.

In the Hebrew Bible, to 'redeem' is something you do for a member of the family. If you are the next of kin, and someone's in trouble, you go and pay the price for them. It's a custom that goes back to people who were so poor that all they had left to give in return for food was themselves, effectively selling themselves into slavery. To say we are 'redeemed' is to say our redeemer is our next of kin, one of our own family, and has settled our account for us, bought us out, rescued us from being slaves to things or people more powerful than we are.

This psalm is about redemption. It lists a range of different situations from which people have been saved. There are as many different places in which people can be redeemed as there are people to be redeemed. In verse 4 there's the wilderness, the desert, a place of famine and thirst. God reaches them there. In verse 10 there's the 'deep shadowy darkness', reminding us of the 'Pit', the grave or prison, as in Psalm 88. God catches hold of them there too. In verse 17 there's the backdrop of sinfulness, of being in the wrong place – this is an imagined setting rather than a geographical location. There too God can reach them to save them. In verse 23 there's the sea, and people being tossed around on its stormy surface. God can reach them there too, because he has power over all creation, even the sea.

Each scene, like a photo-book, shows humanity at the mercy of something more powerful than itself. This translation brings out the clear structure: it's a song with individual verses and then a familiar chorus (like the hymn 'How great thou art'). The verses we've left out – it's a long psalm – describe the paradise-like land where God gives the redeemed a home.

The repeated words – those in *italics* – highlight what these snapshots have in common. Each group of people in trouble calls upon God, and he brings help. The next verse describes the particular help God gives in each setting; then there's another refrain. The Psalmist directs these redeemed people to praise God, to give thanks.

This is the first praise psalm we've looked at. (Scholars try to classify psalms into types, genres or 'forms'; lament is one, praise another.) There have been fragments of praise so far, but this is sustained praise. Lent is a time of fasting and deprivation, penitence and sorrow, disciplines equivalent to the camel-hair shirt John the Baptist wore (Matthew 3; Mark 1). But life is never that simple or dualistic. It's neither perfectly good nor perfectly bad. Every cloud has a silver lining. Even in dark places, a shadow hints that, somewhere, there is something lighter. Black humour finds something to laugh at even when life seems wretched. Storms have centres of calm. Even in the grimmest times, then, there is a mixture. Praise and lament go hand in hand. Emotions are knotty things.

With all these different settings, there's scope for suffering and rescue every time.

A first aid course teaches us how to call for help – even in remote places where there's no mobile phone coverage (or so we think), somehow we can nearly always still make a call. There's always the worry that we'll be out of reach, but the Psalmist's lesson here is: It's not like that with God. He is always within arm's length.

The sea picture is the climax, the culmination of these extreme situations. This is the most remote place imaginable, and so the Psalmist says (verse 24) that especially here can God's saving work be seen for what it is. That's where his 'awesome works' are most evident. Were miracles just a thing of Bible times? No: the Psalmist points us today to look out for these 'awesome works', wonderful deeds, miracles, in every setting where we find ourselves. We are to be as aware of God's saving work as those sailors stranded in the middle of the sea, with no land or security in sight. Even then God steadied them.

We talk about being 'all at sea' if we're overwhelmed by life, a bit lost. Perhaps this is the best time really to spot God. A candle in sunshine is barely noticeable, but a candle in a cellar or during a power cut radiates light.

It's the same with God's miracles, especially the miracle of his 'loving-kindness'. This Hebrew word *hesed* occurs regularly throughout the Old Testament. It's the most obvious way to point out that the God of the New Testament is the same as the God of the Old Testament. This is steadfast, unchanging love; covenant love – and God does not break the covenant. As he sums up at the end, the Psalmist says that this is what it is to be wise – to understand God's loving-kindness. There's no place it can't reach.

The Psalmist often gives reasons – why God should help, why people should praise God. Psalm 107 is a hard-hitting list pointing us to praise.

*What's the most extreme praise you can imagine offering God?*

# Wednesday

## ... to the heavens

---

## Psalm 8

1   For the worship leader: on The Gittith.
    A psalm of David.
    O Yahweh, our Lord! How majestic is your name in all the
    world! Because you set your glory above the heavens!
2   Out of the mouth of children and the young you have
    established strength because of those who are hostile to you,
    to restrain the enemy and the avenger.
3   When I see the heavens, the works of your fingers, the moon
    and the stars that you have created,
4   what is humankind, that you remember us, the son of man
    that you are attentive to us?
5   You have made mankind only a little less than God, and you
    have crowned mankind with glory and honour.
6   You have given mankind authority over the works of your
    two hands, and you have put everything beneath the foot of
    mankind:
7   flocks and oxen, all of them; also the animals of the land;
8   the birds of the sky, the fishes of the sea, all that crosses the
    paths of the seas.
9   O Yahweh, our Lord! How majestic is your name in all the
    world!

Yesterday we read our first praise psalm this Lent. Our reading
today, Psalm 8, is the first praise psalm in the Psalter. God is always
the focus, the conversation partner. The psalm is remarkably

undistracted. Often in psalms, the speaker skips around – from addressing God, to addressing other people, to addressing himself. We know how easily we can be distracted when we're praying or in church. We think about what we've got to do next, worry about something. One moment we're praying, the next we're planning a new project. How does that happen? It can be very frustrating. We can't keep our minds on God. But in Psalm 8, there is a wonderful constancy – complete, wholehearted absorption in God. That's a really precious gift for us in our prayers.

Another precious gift is that God attends to both large and small. From the sea in Psalm 107, now we look to the heavens (verse 1). God is universal (as in Psalm 2) – majestic in all the world, above the heavens – but also specific, caring about the tiny details of infant lives. There are broad-brush strokes and delicate touches. The picture of children too small to speak (verse 2) expresses intimacy between God and mankind. It's a physical, fleshly, incarnate way of talking; a Christmas way of thinking about God. God commits himself even to a baby.

This pattern of zooming in and out carries on. One moment the Psalmist sees the awesome horizons of God's world, the next he sees God close up. Then, taking his attention from the night sky (verse 3), he concentrates his awed gaze on humanity and himself. 'What am I . . .?' he asks (verse 4). He sees himself against the backdrop of the heavens and the whole earth. He marvels. He brings us into this wonder too. This is about all his brothers and sisters, all humanity.

The Psalmist sings God's praises openly: he wants others to join in. He doesn't force himself upon them, however; he addresses no one but God. His witness to God, his personal awe before God, is infectious; enviably so.

Hebrew poetry uses pairs of words or phrases, like 'mankind' and 'the son of man' (verse 4), to express one idea with real emphasis. God cares for both, because they're one and the same, just in different words. The 'son of man' can mean a kind of 'Joe Bloggs', 'everyman', or 'each and every one' – as well as a kind of divine human (look at Daniel 7.14). Jesus uses it in Aramaic to refer to himself. The phrase draws everyone together, showing care even for the individual. One and all, big or small, God is concerned with us.

There's also togetherness in the music group imagined in the psalm heading. We've seen a few superscriptions like this already. We're not told precisely what the tune, or instrument, or style of music 'The Gittith' was, but this is unquestionably a song for public worship. The Psalmist-as-worship-leader is sharing his music, his praise, letting others claim that song for themselves. As at traditional choral services today, the choir does most of the singing but the words and praise are ours as much as they belong to the singers, or to others, past, present and future.

That's quite a community! The Psalmist gives us all responsibility to join in with that ancient congregation, making sure that worship carries on. Humanity across the ages is drawn again into relationship with God, humanity's maker, the source and object of human wonder.

We're related to all of creation. 'You have put everything beneath the foot of mankind' (verse 6). The Psalmist proclaims to God what God already knows. He's telling God that he looks up to him as the Creator of life, who orders the universe; he's saying he knows his own place within creation. The Psalmist makes himself small and big at the same time.

We have responsibilities to be both small and big: humble in relationship to our Creator, dutiful in relationship to all other creatures, 'not to hide ourselves from our own kin' (Isaiah 58.7). This is our right place in this ordered universe. Like the Psalmist, we are to look upon God with awe, and praise him; we are to be responsible *to* and *for* all the works of God's hands. The worship leader praises God – and teaches us.

He retells the creation story – in reverse. Human authority in God's creation echoes Genesis 1.26, the last words of the sixth day of the first creation story (Genesis 1—2.3). In verse 7, the Psalmist makes us think of the first words of that sixth day of creation, when God created flocks, oxen and animals of the land (Genesis 1.24–25). In verse 8, the birds, fish and sea creatures recall the fifth day of creation (Genesis 1.20–22). Finally, verse 9 takes us back to where we started: God.

Creature relates to Creator. We talk of 'creatures' as creepy-crawlies we come across when cleaning. We affectionately call a child a 'little creature' or 'cheeky monkey'. But we're all creatures. We are little too, and we need wisdom to look after a world where climate change is pressing. It's not just the job of the politicians or scientists. We're all to keep learning about our universe. It's an immense creation. Psalm 8 teaches us afresh through prayer and praise to be mindful of the great world around us, learning to take seriously our responsibilities within it, tiny players within a massive – and growing – universe.

Psalm 8 plays with size. God's perspective from above the heavens is vast. But he cares so much about his own creation that he gets close up. In Jesus, he puts himself right in the dust with us all. It's a big world, but God is bigger. Yet it's also a small world: we glimpse God on our own level.

When we know our true size, that's when we really grow.

*How big are you?*

# Thursday

## *God my rock*

———◆◦◆———

### Psalm 18.1–20, 47–51

1   For the Director of Music. Of the Servant of the Lord, of David, who sang to the Lord the words of this song on the day the Lord delivered him from the hand of all his enemies, and from the hand of Saul.

2   And he said, 'I adore you, Lord my strength!'

3   O Lord, my crag and my strong place, you have delivered me, my God, my rock when I am looking for refuge, my shield, my means of calling for salvation, my retreat!

4   You are praiseworthy for all this! I called to the Lord and from my enemy was I saved.

5   Ropes of death encompassed me, and torrents of worthlessness terrified me.

6   Cords of hell entangled me, death-traps confronted me.

7   In my distress I called upon the Lord, I cried to God to help me. In his Temple, he heard my voice, and my cry for help reached his ears.

8   With the earth shaking and quaking, the very foundations of the mountains were rocked, they shook because anger was burning in him.

9   Smoke went up from his nostrils, and fire from his mouth, devouring coals burst burning from him.

10   He stretched the sky low and came down, and heavy cloud was beneath his feet.

11   He mounted an angelic creature and flew; he swept down on the wings of the wind.

12  He set darkness as his screen; his pavilion all around him was
     thick clouds dark with water.
13  Out of the brightness before him, dark clouds came, hail and
     fiery coals.
14  The LORD thundered from the heavens; the Most High gave his
     voice – hail and fiery coals.
15  He let fly his arrows and scattered them; great bolts of
     lightning and vexed them.
16  The channels of the ocean were exposed, the foundations of
     the world were uncovered at your rebuke, O LORD, at the blast
     of the breath of your nostrils.
17  He reached down from on high, he took me, he drew me out
     from the mighty waters.
18  He saved me from my powerful enemy, from those who hate
     me, because they were too strong for me.
19  They confronted me on the day when it all went wrong for
     me, but the LORD was my support.
20  He brought me out into a spacious place, and he delivered me,
     because he delighted in me.

47  The LORD lives! Blessed be my rock! May he be exalted, God,
     my saviour!
48  The God who gives me vengeance and makes people subject
     to me,
49  who rescued me from my enemies, indeed from my opponents
     you have lifted me clear, you have saved me from violent men.
50  And so let me praise you, O LORD, among the peoples, and let
     me make music to your name!
51  He makes great the victories of his king, and he upholds
     his loving-kindness to his anointed, to David and to his
     descendants for ever.

So creation is big, awesome and effectively untameable, beyond our
own experienced places, from the sea to the heavens. Much of Psalm
18 talks about the wildness and power of creation, connecting it
with God.

There's a saying in English about 'being caught between a rock and a hard place'. It's about being stuck, constrained, trapped between two equally difficult alternatives. It conjures up the setting of a wilderness where all that matters are these two rocky, cliff-like places. Rocks can feel threatening: the red-hot rocks spewed out of volcanoes; the rock of the ocean bed that is torn apart in an earthquake and the consequent tsunami.

We can't even trust rocks to be solid. Yes, there was Jesus' story about two houses, one built on sand, the other on rock; a storm easily destroyed the first, but the second had good foundations (Matthew 7; Luke 6). He wanted people to build their lives on the strong and faithful foundation of God. But there's also the possibility of something being a bit rocky. Climbing on rocks at the seaside or around ancient ruins can be exciting but dangerous: rocks can tumble as easily as a person can tumble on them. Like uneven pavements or potholes, rocks can trip us up. But rocks can also be used as pillows in the desert. Rocks have a certain independence: they are valuable in all sorts of different ways, and should be respected.

There are other places in the Bible where rocks crop up. In particular Jesus' disciple and – in latter days – apostle, Peter, who used to be called Simon. By calling him Peter instead, Jesus was calling him both 'the rock' and 'rocky' (Matthew 16). A crucial building block of the future Church, he too could wobble – he famously denied Jesus on the night before the crucifixion.

Jesus knew that rocks were important to the Jews: rocks were part of their landscape, both physically and spiritually. Psalm 18 is one place in the Hebrew Bible where that's particularly evident. The Psalmist calls God his 'crag', his 'rock' (verse 3), meaning a strong position, a safe place, a high-up vantage point, a place of power and refuge.

Psalm 18 connects with another part of the Hebrew Bible. The text of 2 Samuel 22 is very similar, and the superscription to the psalm gives it the same context: a psalm that David sang when God rescued him from all his enemies, including Saul. It seems that the Psalmist and the writer of 2 Samuel at the very least shared a tradition, and knew the same texts and prayers. This happens from time to time in the Old Testament – something you find in one place also appears in almost identical terms somewhere else. That means that sometimes when phrases or texts from the Old Testament are referenced in the New Testament, the New Testament writers were following a Jewish mindset: the Hebrew Scriptures were part of their language, shaping the way they thought about the world and God. 'God is my rock' is a good example of this.

Rocks form a prominent backdrop to this psalm. There are rocks at the high places and on the craggy ridges, rocks at the very bottom of the mountains and the foundations of the earth – and of course the Temple where God resides is crafted of beautiful stone hewn from the rocks. God can be present on all these levels. Just as in Psalm 107, where there's nowhere God can't rescue us from, so here too God's power is evident everywhere. Even in the rocks that are so deep down in the earth we can't fathom them, or those that are on such remote mountain peaks we can't reach them. God is the sturdy material that makes up the foundation of all the earth. That's worthy of blessing and praise.

The dramatic, almost apocalyptic images in Psalm 18 describe a host of natural disasters. There are overtones of floods: verses 5–6 are remembered in Jonah's prayer while in the belly of the fish in the middle of the sea (Jonah 2), and the bottom of the sea and the mighty waters are present in verses 16–17. The words evoke tsunamis, and the destruction they bring. Verse 8 uses the image of a great earthquake, and the smoke, fire, hot coals and dark clouds depict the eruption of a volcano. The heavy clouds, pouring rain, hail and lightning intertwined with all this are emblems of a terrific storm.

The natural world can be vicious, violent, terrifying. If we ever think we have harnessed its power, we should realize how little of that power we've actually recognized. Natural disasters wait for no one. If we are lucky we can escape them or minimize their risks; yet the poor have no option but to live in dangerous places where natural disasters are a part of daily existence – they are literally living on the edge.

Remember what a big world this is, what an immense creation surrounds us. But above all, remember that God is at the very heart of this creation. Ancient writers likened him to the solid stuff that constitutes its very foundations. He can constitute our foundations too.

*Touch the most solid thing you have to hand. What does it mean to be solid?*

# *Friday*

## *A world in worship*

---

## Psalm 65

1   For the Director of Music. A psalm of David. A song.
2   Praise awaits you, O God, in Zion, and vows to you will be fulfilled,
3   you who hear prayer, to you will all humanity come.
4   When our record of wrongdoing is too great for me, it is you who make amends for our errors.
5   Blessed is he whom you choose and you bring near so that he dwells in your courts! May we be filled with the goodness of your house – your holy Temple.
6   Your awesome deeds, fulfilled in righteousness, are your answer to us, O God our salvation, the confidence of all the ends of the earth and the farthest sea.
7   You set in place the mountains by your might, you who are girded in strength.
8   You still the roaring of the seas, the roaring of their waves, and tumultuous peoples.
9   They are afraid, those who live at the ends of the earth, awed by your wonders; the eastern lands of the sunrise and the western lands of the sunset, you make them shout with joy.
10   You pay attention to the earth and you water it, you enrich it greatly with the channel of God filled with water. You have made corn grow for them, for this is how you have established it.
11   Saturating its furrows, flattening it where it has been ploughed, with abundant rain showers you soften the ground and you bless its growth.

12   You crown the year with your goodness, your farm tracks drip
     with abundance.
13   The habitable parts of the desert are also dripping, and the hills
     are clothed with rejoicing.
14   The pastures are covered with sheep, and the vales are
     blanketed with corn; they shout, and even break into song.

'It's a small world', we might say casually when we're chatting with someone we've only just met, and we discover we have mutual friends. Our horizons are limited by our surroundings and the little worlds we create for ourselves – our homes, social groups, workplace, neighbourhoods, the people we have things in common with.

It is all too easy to have limited vision, to create our own cosy worlds where we're at the centre. But then along comes something which jars us out of that. Perhaps the messiness of family, young or old, who need us encroaches on our tidy work life. The needs of people we normally try not to think about suddenly press in on us. Our own sickness or trials set us whirling. We're reminded that we're not the be-all and end-all of the world, we notice afresh that we can't control everything, and we realize that in the wider world, it's just not about *us*.

Psalms reminding us how *big* the world is help us stop and think about our smallness within the world, the fact that we're rather small fish in a big pond.

God is for all humanity (verse 3). God cares as much about the people we avoid as about those we love. His salvation and his blessings are for people we've never even known about, faraway peoples whose cultures and lives we can't begin to understand (verse 9). God is our God. Not just my God, not just my friends' God, not just my church's God, but God of the whole of humanity, God of the whole world.

Opening up our horizons daily, we see anew the apparently crazy picture of St Francis preaching to the birds. Kitsch representations of a holy man surrounded by beautiful creatures constitute the popular image of a saint whose social cares and deep humanity Pope Francis brought to the world's attention. This image speaks volumes when it's less domesticated. St Francis' care for creatures was such that he saw our value to God, and understood how we as the whole of creation are called into relationship with God. So in his songs he addressed all creatures – even the cosmic and elemental – envisaging us all joining in the praises of God. God is so worthy of praise that it still wouldn't be enough even if the whole universe were to join together in blessing our Creator! That's why he needed to preach to the birds. This message can also be Francis' lesson to us.

And it is the Psalmist's lesson to us in Psalm 65. God here pays attention to the ends of the earth and the details of its nourishment (verse 10). The cultivated fields, irrigation channels, cart tracks, pastures, as well as the mountains, oceans, deserts, and lands of the farthest east and west where the sun rises and sets: it's God's richness that makes all these places fruitful. God attends to all parts of his great creation. Here's another message: however small we are in this big world, there is a reason for confidence. In the world the Psalmist describes, there is goodness pouring out in all sorts of different places.

This sets us a challenge. Where do we see the goodness, the abundant fruitfulness of God, in cities brought to rubble by warfare or natural disaster? The Psalmist only talks of the 'habitable parts of the desert' (verse 13). He's not trying to give us an unrealistic view of an entire world dripping with food and abundance. There are other parts of the world that go beyond even his imagining, his travel catalogue.

That doesn't mean that God doesn't care about them. The Psalmist doesn't tackle the most difficult terrain here, because the picture he gives is of not being able to hold back from praising God. This praise is an infectious desire to worship. Richer, more developed countries and places have two things to hear. First, those who have the most also have most responsibility to praise God, to bless him for fruitfulness. And second, those in affluent parts of the world should reflect on what abundance truly is, and where true riches are really to be found. After all, in the Gospels, Jesus often suggests that in his kingdom, the so-called 'rich' will actually have the toughest time.

The final verse dedicates this psalm to the whole of creation. That last word, 'song', is the last word of the opening verse too. This psalm is a particular kind of song (Hebrew has lots of different words for songs and psalms); it's exactly this kind of song that the Psalmist hears the pastures and the vales singing.

Water helps the song flow. Verses 10 to the end are green and verdant because God waters the earth, as he does in so many traditional harvest hymns. But water is richer than even this: it is a symbol of the Spirit of God, and it is what flows from the side of the crucified Christ. We can be like well-watered countryside, drinking in God's Spirit and blossoming with praise.

*What makes you grow and sing?*

# Saturday

## Nothing is beyond God

———◦•◦———

## Psalm 139

¹  For the Director of Music. Of David. A psalm.
   O LORD, you have searched me, and you know me.

²  You know when I sit down and when I stand up, you understand
   my aim even from far away.

³  You measure my walking and my lying down, you are familiar
   with all my ways.

⁴  For there is not a word on my tongue that you don't already
   know, O LORD.

⁵  Behind me and in front of me, you secure me; you lay your
   hand on me.

⁶  This knowledge is too amazing for me to get my head around;
   it is simply too elevated for me!

⁷  Where may I go where I would be away from your spirit? And
   where may I run away to from your presence?

⁸  If I ascend to heaven, there you are! and if I lie down in hell,
   look, there you are again!

⁹  If I were to rise up on wings of the dawn and if I were to settle
   down on the other side of the sea,

¹⁰  even there your hand would be guiding me, and your right
   hand holding me steady.

¹¹  If I say, 'Surely darkness will cover me, and light become night
   all around me,'

¹²  darkness is not too dark for you to see, night is just as light as
   the day. Like darkness, like light!

13 For they even belong to you, my mind and my heart; you wove me together in my mother's womb.

14 Let me praise you, because, amazingly, I am made as a living miracle; your deeds are marvels, and my soul knows that intimately.

15 My skeleton was not hidden from you when I was made in a hidden place, when I was clothed in the depths of the earth.

16 Even my embryonic form, your eyes saw it; on your scroll every one of my days was written, they were part of your plan, each one of them.

17 How precious are your purposes for me, O God! How many they are in total!

18 If I were to count them, they would be many, many more than the grains of sand. I come to the end, and still I am with you.

19 If only, O God, you would kill the wicked! Get away from me, bloody men!

20 They speak of you only to get their own way, they honour you with empty hearts, that's what your foes do.

21 O LORD, don't I hate those who hate you, and loathe those who try to raise themselves up to your heights?

22 I hate, hate them completely, they have become enemies to me also!

23 Examine me intently, O God, and know what I think; cross-examine me and know my secrets.

24 See if I go after anything else but you, and lead me in the way of eternity.

Our psalms this week have pointed to how God attends to the ends of the earth as well as the detail in many different settings. There are similar horizons in Psalm 139. What really comes out in this psalm however is *knowledge*. God's knowledge of us is, always has been and always will be entire and true. Our knowledge of God on the other hand can increase, and as it does, it draws us closer to God in prayer and praise.

God knows us inside out. From the hairs on our heads to the soles of our feet, from the inmost recesses of our psyche to our most obvious outward acts and appearances, God's 'got us sussed'. That's inevitable, since he was involved in our earliest moments of creation, and there's nowhere we can be without him, like it or not.

Knowledge is there right at the start, and it's repeated in the parallelism in the penultimate verse 23. In verses 1–6 the Psalmist ponders God's great knowledge of him. Is there anything God doesn't know? he asks. That's awesome . . . God's more aware of me than I am myself. He knows what I'm thinking, what I'm doing, what I'm saying, where I'm going, what I'm writing now or what you're reading.

Remembering that God knows all the secrets of our hearts, as in Psalm 50, keeps us close to God. It challenges us: it helps to keep us on the straight and narrow, to be as thoughtful about what we do as God is thoughtful about us. It comforts us: we know that, whatever faces us, God's in it with us.

There's utter delight in realizing the presence of God. In verse 8, the Psalmist plays childlike peeping games. The fun, jocund tone carries on: in verse 12, 'Like darkness, like light' is similar to our phrase 'Like mother, like daughter'. The Psalmist is saying that some differences can always be transcended: darkness or light, it makes no difference to God.

God knows all this before we will (verses 13–18). The Psalmist considers our gradual creation as human beings, building us up from the vital organs at our centre (verse 13), putting flesh on our skeletons (verse 15). Nothing about us can be hidden from God, either in place (our mother's womb) or in time (before we were conceived). This is intricate creation and intimate knowledge.

God had plans for each of us as embryos. It is so bold a thought that it blows the Psalmist's mind. Just imagine: if that's the case, then God has thought about astonishing details in our lives. Like the 'butterfly effect', where the flutter of a butterfly's wings has an impact on what's happening the other side of the world, small causes can lead to big outcomes. So God really does know all the tininess of our lives as well as the bigger picture. The picture of the grains of sand (verse 18) points to the many tiny things God knows and cares about in our lives. God promises the childless Abraham as many offspring as grains of sand (Genesis 22). Grains of sand describe an immeasurable number. The idea that God has this many plans for us, big and small, is an immensely precious thought.

But then the Psalmist comes up against a problem. If God knows all this, and cares so much, how come there are people having a go at me? How does that fit into God's plan? The next four verses (19–22) are a huge shock after such beautiful, playful, trusting language and thoughts. The Psalmist is suddenly cursing, swearing at his enemies.

Maybe that's entirely natural. Sometimes people like to ignore these verses because they are too vicious, they don't fit into the gentleness of the rest of the psalm. But they are absolutely to the point. If we believe that God does have a plan for us, that he knows us intimately, cares for us, has done and always will, how on earth do the 'baddies' of this world fit into that plan? How can we make sense of life when things go wrong, when we suffer at the hands of others?

The Psalmist tries to rationalize by saying that his enemies (verse 19) are his enemies because they are God's enemies (verses 20–22). They are rebelling against God's plan for them. Unlike the Psalmist, they are not trying to stay close to God. Their own thoughts, not God's thoughts, are their idols. Their agenda is what matters to them, not what matters to God. Their agenda seems to be to oppose the Psalmist.

Such theodicy, exploring God's justice and trying to explain how suffering can happen, is common in the Psalms, generally whenever enemies come on the scene. As Psalm 139 turns to justice towards its end, it naturally closes with language that could be used in a trial.

The Psalmist's language of examination in the final two verses is fitting for Lent. Asking God to check out our motives, our intentions, bringing us closer to his plan for us, hints that we may not be so different from our sworn enemies after all. Getting close to God means knowing ourselves better. And as we get close to God, he gets close to us: nothing about us is beyond God's power to change if we let him.

*What is your favourite verse in this psalm, and why?*

# WEEK 4

It's a beautiful world

# Monday

## The joy of refreshment

---

**Psalm 23**

¹  A psalm of David. The LORD is my shepherd. I lack nothing.
²  He makes me stretch out in grassy places, he leads me to restful waters.
³  He gives me my life back. He guides me down the right paths for the sake of his name.
⁴  Yes, even in those times when I walk through a valley of deep darkness, I am not afraid of evil, for you are with me; your rod and your staff, they comfort me.
⁵  You set out a table for me, in front of my enemies; you anoint my head with oil; my glass is filled.
⁶  Surely goodness and loving-kindness will pursue me all the days of my life, and I shall live in the house of the LORD for my whole lifetime.

We all need time off, time away from our usual concerns. Yesterday, Mothering Sunday, is also known as 'Refreshment Sunday': a day in the middle of Lent when the mood lightens a little. That's why, symbolically, some churches change the colour of their decorations on that day from deep purple to pink. The joy of Mothering Sunday reminds us that every Sunday, even in Lent, is a feast day to celebrate the resurrection of Christ, a holy day, or 'holiday'.

In Psalm 23, the Psalmist is taking refreshment, having a blissful lie down on soft grass beside a stream or pool. He experiences beauty through all his senses. Alongside the gentle touch of the grass beneath him, the murmur of lightly flowing water, the sight of greenery, he imagines the anticipation of good food with all its delicious smells and tastes, as at a banquet prepared lovingly for him by none other than God himself.

Many ancient poets wrote 'pastoral' poetry, or 'bucolics', simple songs sung as if by shepherds to keep themselves entertained in those long hours on the mountainside watching over their flocks or herds. They might accompany those songs on crude pipes or penny whistles. Perhaps then the Psalmist hasn't actually taken a day off, but is finding rest even in the middle of his tasks and responsibilities. His restfulness is in his experience of the present moment, and in his mind's eye, devoted to God. God's care for him is central to the picture.

God is called a shepherd, both here and elsewhere in the Bible. Sheep, goats, herds were a long-standing aspect of life for the ancient Israelites. These were frequently nomadic, wandering peoples who would take their flocks around in search of good grazing. Paths, rocky and narrow or smooth and wide, were a natural aspect of their surroundings. How wonderful to come out into a broad place, good pastureland, where they could enjoy the grassy banks as much as their sheep and cows did.

Shepherds, though, weren't merely the gentle, caring people of children's story books. In Jesus' time, shepherds were the outcasts who couldn't come into Jerusalem: smelly people, as wild as the countryside which was their bed and shelter. They carried rough weapons or tools, like the rod and the staff (verse 4), which they used to seize hold of sheep who were in trouble, or to fight off wild animals who posed a risk to their flocks. They could also use them to break the legs of sheep who had wandered off, who had disobeyed the shepherd. By inflicting a temporary injury or disability, the shepherd could teach his sheep to do what he wanted them to do. He could also teach them to trust him. For when the shepherd broke the legs of a sheep, he then had to carry it.

That is the picture of the good shepherd evident in the earliest Christian art. There are caves beneath Rome, which were often the safest meeting places for the first generations of the Church, and where they buried their loved ones. In those catacomb chambers are drawings depicting a figure carrying a sheep over his shoulders, resonant with the truth of the rod and staff.

For all its beauty, the countryside can be wild and inhospitable too. So Mothering Sunday as 'refreshment' isn't joyful for everyone. It's often hard for those who don't have children; those whose mothers have died; those for whom the relationship between parent and child has felt destructive rather than life-giving. The countryside, Mothering Sunday, family relationships: all have the potential not only to be beautiful, but also to be deeply threatening. They're double-edged. Even restful Psalm 23 features the 'valley of deep darkness' and the 'enemies'. Holiness is not fluffy and nice. It is often hardcore reality: the combination of beauty and difficulty, both rocky crevasses and awesome mountain ranges.

God is a real shepherd: a shepherd who faces treachery and danger for and with his sheep; a shepherd who relishes gentle countryside and peaceful pasture among his flocks; a shepherd who abides even on the fringes to be with his creatures. In Ezekiel 34 this good shepherd imagery is connected with King David, whose reign was recorded in the Scriptures as one where people felt secure, protected, and looked over by a responsible king. Good kings were sometimes likened to good shepherds. And God is the good King above all others. It's no surprise then that the Gospel writers portray Jesus as a good shepherd, as well as a king.

Anointing, in verse 5, also develops the connection between shepherd and king. To pour oil on guests' heads at the beginning of a dinner party was the most splendid way of greeting them, making them welcome. It was a very elaborate way of helping them freshen up on arrival. It was how preparations were carried out for banquets in the halls of kings in the ancient Near East. Pouring oil on the head was necessary to anoint kings and priests. So for the Psalmist to claim that God treats him like this is to say that he is regally treated by God: it suggests he has been welcomed into the royal family.

Christians believe that's right: that we are welcomed into God's family. Christ regards as his brothers those who do his will (Matthew 12; Mark 3). Through Christ we become heirs of eternal life. This takes us back to Mothering Sunday. Every day is a Psalm 23 day. Every day of our lives we are welcomed into the best family of all: God's family, where kings and shepherds and sheep are brothers and sisters together. Now that really *is* a beautiful world.

*Who are shepherds in our society?*

# Tuesday

*Heavenly voices*

———•◆•———

## Psalm 19

1    For the Director of Music: A psalm of David.

2    The heavens declare the glory of God, and the expansive sky tells out the work of his hands.

3    One day pours out its proclamations to the next day, and one night to the next night speaks out its knowledge.

4    There is no utterance, there are no spoken words, where their sound goes unheard.

5    The skies' voice carries throughout the whole world, their words among the ends of the earth. In them, God has placed a movable dwelling place for the sun,

6    who is like a bridegroom coming out of his chamber, like a champion who can't wait to run his course.

7    From the ends of the heavens is his starting line, and his circuit is to the far end; there is nothing that its heat does not reach.

8    The Torah of the LORD is perfect, and brings the soul round every time; the law code of the LORD is trustworthy and makes the simple wise.

9    The instructions of the LORD are fair and gladden the heart; the commands of the LORD are clear and make the eyes light up.

10    The fear of the LORD is pure and endures for ever; the judgements of the LORD are true, righteous altogether.

11    They are more desirable than gold, than lots of twenty-four-carat gold; they are sweeter than honey, even as it drips overflowing from the comb.

<sup>12</sup> Yes, your servant is directed by them, great are the consequences in following them.

<sup>13</sup> Who spots their own errors? Forgive me for those things I have done wrong and did not notice.

<sup>14</sup> Help your servant to avoid proud sins; may they not get the better of me! Then I shall be whole and I shall be free of disastrous wrongdoing.

<sup>15</sup> May they be for good, the words of my mouth and the musing of my heart in your sight, O Lord, my rock and my redeemer.

'The heavens are telling' is a piece of classical music, part of a longer choral work, *The Creation*, which Joseph Haydn wrote in 1803. The words of the Psalms have been set to all sorts of different styles of music, whether in the context of worship or secular performance, in films, concerts, even pop videos. Many musicians, from Beethoven to Boney M, have been inspired by this psalm. It's incredible to think how much influence so many psalms have across the world's cultures today. That's sure testament to what powerful texts they have always been, and how worthwhile it is to read and re-read them, and live by them. There are many more psalms in the soundtrack of our lives than probably any of us notice.

Psalm 19 depicts praise of God as the soundtrack to day and night, a continuous cosmic hymn. The music of the spheres (verses 2–5) – although we don't actually hear the 'song' of the universe as we would listen to an audio track – has its own rhythm, tune and harmony. Just as we aren't always aware of the recurrent beats of the psalms in our day-to-day existence, so we wouldn't really know the great music of the heavens and the movements of the universe. Psalm 19 draws our attention to this cosmic melody, opening our ears to its message.

That cosmic proclamation unfolds into praise about God's law, the Torah. This divine instruction book was given to Moses centuries ago, after the Israelites escaped slavery in Egypt after the plagues, crossed the Red Sea, and went wandering for 40 long years in the surrounding deserts. The exodus story was central to Jewish understanding of their history and how they came to know themselves as the people God came to save. This was when God gave Moses the Ten Commandments, the beginning of the Jewish Law which was known as the Torah. So the Torah is special, divine teaching.

Naturally then, the heavens' good news is in praise of the Torah. Each of verses 8–10 are made up of two balanced half-verses describing the law in a number of different ways, before the crowning verse 11 describes how desirable it is to have the law and follow it. It is as valuable as today's 24-carat gold (the best gold in the ancient Near East was believed to come from Ophir, which is what the Hebrew actually says). It is as sweet and pleasurable as honey taken fresh from the beehive (honey was as much, if not more, of a delight then as it is now).

That guidance, if we can but follow it, will make us perfect, says the Psalmist. Then, towards the end (verses 13–14), it dawns on him that he probably has not reached those standards, and there's a risk he never will: because his mistakes are much bigger than he even realizes. Therefore he also needs God's help to spot all his errors, so he can keep trying harder. Only then does he stand a chance of being whole, fully healthy – spiritually, emotionally, psychologically – and above all of being in a right relationship with God (another way of understanding what 'righteousness' means).

To Christians, the heavenly message about God's guidance and instruction is a gospel message, the good news of the God who creates, the Lord who saves. God set the planets in their courses, and the Psalmist in verses 6–7 playfully portrays the sun as a champion, like an Olympic athlete, who can't wait to get off the starting blocks each morning to glory in the running of the daily race. Races, like the race of life, become a more common image in the books of the New Testament, especially in letters like those of St Paul, who would have known well the traditions of the Olympics and other ancient series of games.

To a Christian reader, the way that God sets the earth, sun and moon in motion, the way that God tries to keep the creation on track, is first by the Torah and second by Jesus, the Rabbi who was so steeped in the Jewish Law that he could explain it to others. Jesus said he came to fulfil the law, an idea St Paul particularly explores in Romans and Galatians. Knowing that the law was in fact too demanding for you and me to keep day to day, we needed something to make up for us what we couldn't manage by ourselves.

We come back to humility. We can't succeed in living up to God's standards by ourselves. We understand afresh how important Jesus is. The Psalmist prayed that God would forgive him all the faults he wasn't even aware of. Today that prayer can be ours too. But it's not only cause for lament that we've gone astray and persistently get things wrong. It's also praise of Jesus, who came to fulfil the law for us, who bore the extreme physical punishment of the broken laws and teaching of God, by dying wretchedly on the cross even though he had done nothing to deserve it.

That, for Christians, is how true righteousness, or being right with God, is achieved. It's not achieved by us, because we'll never quite make it by ourselves. It's achieved for us by Jesus.

*What is the soundtrack to your life?*

# Wednesday

## God our help

---

### Psalm 121

1 A song for ascents. I lift my eyes up to the mountains. From where comes my help?

2 My help comes from the Lord, the Creator of heaven and earth.

3 May he let not your foot be unsteady, may the one who keeps watch for you not nod off to sleep.

4 Look, the one who keeps watch for Israel does not doze, he does not sleep!

5 The Lord is the one who keeps watch for you, he is the very shadow of your right hand.

6 By day, the sun will not burn you, nor the moon strike you by night.

7 The Lord will keep watch for you from every bad thing; he keeps watch over your soul.

8 The Lord will keep watch over your going out and your coming in, now and for ever.

We've noticed that the Psalms sometimes appear in some kind of order, like Psalms 1 and 2. There are also points within the Psalter where psalms are grouped together.

The 'songs of ascents' form one such collection. Psalms 120–134 are referred to as 'ascents'. We've already looked at Psalm 120. People often ask what 'ascents', or 'goings up' or 'steps up', actually means. Is it a spiritual ascent, a growth in holiness? Or a physical ascent, standing on the steps of the very first Temple in Jerusalem and singing one psalm on each step? Is it a physical progression like going on a pilgrimage? Or a musical direction, to sing each song a little higher in pitch?

Whatever makes sense of the titles for us, what is clear is that these 15 psalms have some things in common. They are fairly short, domestic and homely. They are generally quite upbeat. Psalm 120 is the only one that sounds distressed. Other than that, throughout the collection are a few scattered verses about enemies or hard times. Much more common are images of children, the household, the kitchen table, a basic farming existence that may be hard work but provides good food and a secure settlement. These psalms speak of contentment and safety. They're refreshing after the Lenten laments – and they build up a picture of a world made beautiful by security, happiness and simple pleasures.

That security is largely brought about in Psalm 121 by the kindly God who is watching over the people. He's a God who is alert for their wellbeing, who doesn't doze off and fail to notice that they're running into trouble, or that there's a threat just round the corner. He's the most dependable watchman of a city, the security guard who's ready to deal with any problems.

God's vantage point is high up. The Psalmist early in the 'ascents' looks up, lifting his eyes to the mountains. It's in the mountains that God can best look down and across his settled people. Notice that unlike that depicted in some psalms, this is not a wandering, nomadic existence, but one much more related to the idea of town or city living. Ancient cities were pretty unlike today's cities – they were not really very large, because the population in general was so much smaller. No big industries, just skilled people who could make things. No cars, just the occasional horse for the very important. No supermarkets, just deep cisterns and storage pits for water and grain. No sprawling suburbs, but fortified city gates.

So God is viewed here as being up in the mountains, where he can have a good view over the city and any routes into it. That's where the real help comes from. God is a watchman, someone who can keep an eye on everything and put a swift end to any threats from outside.

This is a watchman who's very much awake, always on hand. The Hebrew Bible makes many contrasts between God, 'the LORD', the God of the Israelites, and the gods of the surrounding peoples, who could be made from pieces of wood, impotent idols incapable of saving their people. When Elijah challenges Baal to a divine competition and Baal doesn't rise to the occasion, Elijah accuses him of being asleep; then the God of Israel works the hoped-for miracle by sending fire just as Elijah asked (1 Kings 18). Baal is the typical god who sleeps – or perhaps just isn't there at all . . . but the God of Israel is most definitely there, and most certainly alert, as in Psalm 121.

But God isn't just up in the mountains. He's there at every footstep the Psalmist takes, to make sure it is steady (verse 3); he's even the shadow of the Psalmist's right hand (verse 5). There's no slipping on mountain paths here. God looks after us at home and away (verse 8). That's good news for us when we are far from home, or when we are separated from beloved family members or dear friends by miles or even continents.

God, the Creator, is perfectly positioned to look after both the big picture of a whole city and the minute details of everyday life – as we saw in the zooming-in-and-out of Psalm 8 last week.

The liturgical refrain after Easter, between Ascension Day and Pentecost, 'The Spirit of God fills the whole world', encapsulates the ideas of Psalm 121. The Spirit of God, present at creation, is also the Holy Spirit given by Jesus after his resurrection. As in Psalm 139, there's nowhere the Spirit is not, whether we're inside or outside, at home or away.

*Looking up to the horizon, or gazing down upon a beautiful view, what do you notice?*

# Thursday

## *Adorned as a bride*

---

## Psalm 45

1  For the Director of Music. To the tune of 'Lilies'. Of the sons of
   Korah, a song of understanding, a love song.
2  My heart is stirring lovely words, I am composing verses for the
   king, my tongue is the flowing pen of a skilful scribe.
3  You are better looking than any other man. Grace informs
   all you say. Therefore God has given you blessing for ever.
4  Strap your sword to your side, you hero! Your vigour and your
   splendour,
5  your splendour, prosper them! Mount and ride out for the sake
   of truth, and in the cause of righteousness, and may your right
   hand guide you to awesome deeds.
6  With your arrows, sharpened, in the hearts of the king's
   enemies, peoples fall beneath you.
7  Your throne, O God, is for ever and ever, the staff which brings
   about fairness is the staff of your kingly reign.
8  You love what is right and hate what is wrong. Therefore God,
   your God, has anointed you with the oil of gladness over all
   your fellows.
9  Myrrh, aloe vera and botanical fragrance are the scent of all
   your clothes. From ivory-panelled palaces comes the string
   music which makes you smile.
10 Daughters of kings are among your ladies of honour; your
   bride stands at your right hand, wearing the most exotic gold.
11 Listen to this, my girl, and take notice; bend your ear to my
   words: Forget your people and your father's house,

¹² let the king desire your beauty; since this man is your lord, bow to him.

¹³ My Tyrian girl, rich people will try to sweeten you up to their purposes, bringing gifts before you,

¹⁴ all kinds of luxuries. The royal princess, wearing a dress laced with gold,

¹⁵ embroidered delicately, inside is she led to the king. Her maids-in-waiting, behind her, are introduced to you.

¹⁶ They are led in, full of joy and happiness, and they enter the palace of the king.

¹⁷ Instead of your forefathers now will be your sons; you will set them as leaders throughout the whole land.

¹⁸ So may I commemorate your name for each and every generation, so that peoples will sing your praises for ever and ever.

This psalm is another 'Maskil', a 'song of understanding'. It's also a love song, apparently written for a royal wedding. It's unique as a psalm addressed almost entirely to two individuals, the king and the royal princess who is his bride. Only one verse is addressed to God (verse 7), and it connects the justice of God's reign with the right-eousness of the king's reign.

After the heading, the introduction (verse 2) helps us imagine the Psalmist composing this royal eulogy. He's the Poet Laureate of an ancient Near Eastern king. Such an encomium, a poem of praise like this, is composed with care and grace, to be written down as well as sung, to be recorded for future reference. The Psalmist himself likens his oral inventions to the flowing pen of the scribe, who is accurate and trustworthy. This praise, he says, is therefore factually as reliable as the written records made by secretaries to royalty, to be stored in the archives. His message: take this king seriously.

Since this reign is connected with God's own reign, the marriage matters. A good king's marriage could lead to future generations of princes and leaders as reliable and praiseworthy as the present king. The bridegroom is responsible not only for being a wise king right now, but also for having offspring who will do a great job in the future. Both bridegroom and bride need to be strong, beautiful, heroic, capable of producing heirs who can bring security for generations to come.

Not surprisingly then, the royal bridegroom is painted as handsome, with the right words for any occasion, a strong heroic figure whose warlike valour brings justice and dependable defence (verses 3–8). He's in his prime, he has the right opinions and instincts, and his riches – his clothes and palace – are a sure sign of his excellence.

In the ancient Near East, prosperity was often regarded as belonging only to those who deserved it. If you were this wealthy, you must be very good. That's why the royal couple are described as covered in luxurious dress and valuables. On this their wedding day they really have got their finery out. We are invited to smell the bridegroom's highly fragranced clothes (verse 9), to wonder at all the gold, both in the heavy jewellery worn by the princess, and the intricate filigree, the shimmering gold lace of her dress.

Shifting his gaze from the bridegroom to contemplate the princess, the Psalmist moves to address her instead (verses 11 and 13). He thinks how she will never be lacking in luxury and riches, because she will be courted by many people wanting the king's favour. This is a princess from Tyre, who no doubt brought much wealth with her already, but who is now to take one of the most powerful roles any woman could hold. She would have the ear of the king, and be in a position to charm him into her ways of thinking. It would be understandable if people tried to bribe her to do just that, says the Psalmist, subtly warning her of the power she is about to wield (verses 13–14).

Above all, she has her duty: to submit to her bridegroom, the king, and look up to him; to enter the king's chamber, to fulfil her responsibility to bear him children and heirs. The young couple together must look away from their fathers and ancestors, and to the future (verse 17). All those around them furthermore have a duty to support them in this – the beautiful train of the bride's ladies-in-waiting, and the Psalmist himself.

So this joyful psalm is all about planning for the future with such hope (think of the excitement of a big royal wedding in Westminster Abbey). The wedding setting is intriguing within the Psalter as a whole. Whether the psalm was written for a specific marriage, or composed simply as an imagined royal moment, it tells us how such ceremonies might believably have been conducted, what were the concerns of the domestic life of ancient Near Eastern kings, and what was important for the ideal kingly reign.

'Prepared as a bride adorned for her husband': the imagery of the spectacular wedding, bride and bridegroom ready to make their perfect match, features elsewhere in the Hebrew Bible. The beautiful poetry of the Song of Songs (sounding decidedly erotic in some places) has been regarded through the centuries as an apt description of God's love for his people. In the Prophets, marriages signify that the people are doing well, and are a cause for joy; when a city runs into trouble, it can host no wedding parties . . . God's people seem to be failing in their relationship with him.

Jesus and the writers of the New Testament used the wedding party as apocalyptic imagery. Here the perfect wedding is not between a handsome earthly king and a pretty young bride, but between God and his people. The unwise bridesmaids weren't prepared for the arrival of the bridegroom, and so couldn't join in the heavenly party. The best party in the Bible, the wedding at Cana where Jesus turned water into wine (John 2), is a symbolic party foreshadowing the banquet in God's kingdom. The Church in our day too is called to be as a bride adorned for her husband – ready for Jesus to come again and claim us as his own.

*What makes people truly beautiful?*

# Friday

## The beauty of holiness

---

### Psalm 96

1   Sing to the LORD a new song, sing to the LORD, all the earth.
2   Sing to the LORD, bless his name, bear the good news from day
    to day of how he saves.
3   Tell out among the peoples his glory, among all the nations his
    wonderful doings.
4   For great is the LORD and to be praised most awesomely; he is
    above all gods.
5   For all the divinities of the peoples are to be dissed; but the
    LORD made the heavens.
6   Splendour and honour are before him, strength and beauty are
    in his sanctuary.
7   Credit the LORD, you families of the peoples, credit the LORD
    with glory and strength.
8   Credit the LORD with the glory of his name, bring tribute and
    enter his residence.
9   Worship the LORD in honourable holiness; tremble in his presence,
    all the earth!
10  Tell out among the nations, 'The LORD is King!' Indeed, the world
    stands firm, it cannot be shaken; he judges the peoples fairly.
11  Let the skies rejoice, let the earth be happy, let the sea and all
    within it thunder,
12  let the fields and everything in them be jubilant; then all the
    trees of the forest will shout for joy
13  at the presence of the LORD; for he comes, for he comes to rule
    the earth; he will rule the world with righteousness and the
    peoples with a steady hand.

Psalms 96–99 fit together as a mini-collection, alternating songs about God's kingship with hymns, and with shared themes across the four psalms linking them closely.

When God is King, the world is beautiful indeed. We pick this up from the virtues that, for the Psalmist, go along with being a good king. Such a king is glorious, splendid, powerful, mighty, strong, honourable, holy – and above all, righteous. The Hebrew idea of 'judging' is also about 'ruling', so explains the book of Judges, which tells the history of the early leaders of Judah and Israel before the monarchy. Providing justice went along with being in power. It makes sense – you appeal to the highest authority in any kind of dispute, and the most powerful provides the final judgement. Verse 13, linking with verse 10, is a celebration of God's presence among his peoples, even among the whole world, as the most righteous, fairest authority there can be. God provides perfect justice.

This justice is beautiful, both in itself and in the harmony it creates. This is the Creator God, who made even the heavens, the divine dwelling place. It's God's beautiful creation that is rejoicing in verses 11 and 12. It reminds us of Psalm 19, where the natural world knows full well how to praise God and speak out about him.

This is also the responsibility of 'the whole earth', which is addressed clearly in verses 1 and 9. It is God who makes firm, who establishes the entire world (verse 10). The remaining descriptions of creation cover all the details of that created world: peoples the world over, the skies, earth, sea and land, both fields and forests, and all that is in them are also called to praise.

What's more, this truly includes every people. Every country, tribe, nation, continent, island: all of us. The Psalmist challenges us to attribute to God all the greatness that is his (verses 7 and 8). We must give him the credit, acknowledge his glory and power. This God deserves us to treat him as King – to obey him, to look up to him, to work with and to pray for his peaceful and just kingdom.

This matters for all people. All of God's creation is called to sing this new song, to tell out his true kingship. Phrases about 'telling out', or 'declaring', in the Psalms prefigure for the Christian the Magnificat, or 'Mary's Song', which Mary sings when she learns that she is pregnant with the Son of God. Heard at Evensong services the world over today, this song is beautiful, and it's been set to music countless times throughout the millennia, as in, for example, the hymn 'Tell out my soul'. Telling out God's praises is a good way of honouring our King.

What though is the 'new song'? Psalm 96 asserts again that God – the God of Israel – is the God above all other gods; that other gods are to be overlooked. At this early stage of religious development in the ancient world, there's actually no denial that there are other gods, but there is the all-important recognition that other gods don't matter, even if they do exist: the only god who matters, who truly exists, is the Lord God of Israel. So in verse 5 there is the idea that we can shrug, in the way of a truculent teenager or hip student, 'Am I bovvered?' about any god other than the Lord God, this God who is the true King of all. Verse 5 also contains a play on words. The Hebrew language is very fond of wordplays, and I've tried to bring it out by using the complacent youthful word 'dissing' ('disrespecting'), which alliterates with the word 'divinities'.

While thinking about wordplay, it's fascinating to realize that the ancient text would have contained only consonants. Those who knew Hebrew knew which vowels to put into each word so that it all made sense, so the writers left the vowels out. There wouldn't have been punctuation either, so it's up to the translator to work out where to put speech marks. Look at verse 10: is the Psalmist speaking all this, or is he putting some of this song into the voice of 'the whole earth' which he addresses? If so, how much? Whose praise is this – the Psalmist's own praise of God, or the praise he suggests that everyone else join in singing? Who sings what?

Sometimes it can be hard to sing a song of praise. We're not in the mood, we're having difficult times, the last thing we want to do when life feels tough is praise God or give thanks. But we can let the Psalms help us. Today the Psalmist gives us words that we can use to praise God regardless of how we're feeling: the praise is provided for us.

*What do you think is most beautiful about God's kingdom?*

# Saturday

## *The beauty of simplicity*

---

### Psalm 131

¹   A song of ascents. Of David.
   O LORD, my heart is not haughty, and I do not stick my chin in
   the air; I do not get involved in things that are too great or too
   important for me.

²   Rather, I have steadied and quietened my soul, just like a
   weaned child on his mother, like a weaned child on my breast
   is my soul.

³   O Israel, wait faithfully for the LORD, now and for ever.

Sometimes words from the Bible seem to be directed specifically at us. St Augustine (354–430) tells a story of how children chanting 'Pick up and read!' made him turn to his Bible, like other holy people before him, and the words he read there seemed to be precisely those he most needed.

A friend tells how as a young man he wrote a very stroppy letter, and an hour later he was preparing with his choir to sing Evensong. It was Psalm 131. With a sinking spirit he realized his earlier actions had been haughty, stuck up, and that he had addressed a senior with discourtesy and pride. As the choir rehearsed he reflected on the words and before he had been summoned to answer for his letter, he already knew he had done just as the Psalmist was encouraging him not to do.

Pride and a high opinion of ourselves lead to mistakes, often big ones. By grace alone can we avoid pressing 'send' on an email in response to something that's wound us up. By grace alone can we hold back from our self-righteous ranting, probe gently, and listen to what was behind a particular episode. These are habits of humility.

Psalm 131 reminds us of the simple pleasure of not getting too deeply involved in things that aren't really for us to wade into. This Psalmist has stopped strutting around full of himself and busying himself with things that are actually beyond him, his position or his pay grade. He no longer holds forth in conversation with his great opinions because, in fact, he doesn't have the responsibility or expertise to offer the answer to the world's problems.

Pride in who we think we are is destructive. It leads us to lie to ourselves, to those we love, and ultimately to God. We should certainly give that up for Lent, and for our whole lives. It is hard to let go of, but once we do, and regularly prevent ourselves picking it up again, the burden released helps us to realize who we *really* are. Children loved by God. Nothing more, nothing less.

That takes us back to humility. Here in Psalm 131 it's clear it involves real self-awareness and recognition of our true size in the whole world around us. There are many things that are too big for us, that we shouldn't pretend or kid ourselves that we can actually do anything about.

Humility is basic to life. The Principles of the Anglican Franciscans have some helpful things to say about humility. Like this:

> Humility confesses that we have nothing that we have not received and admits the fact of our insufficiency and our dependence on God. It is the basis of all Christian virtues. Saint Bernard of Clairvaux said, 'No spiritual house can stand for a moment except on the foundation of humility'. It is the first condition of a joyful life within any community.

Alongside Psalm 131, these words chime with the image in verse 2 of the weaned child peaceful on his mother's breast. He is content in his smallness and his dependency. Just so, says the Psalmist, is his own soul within him. He is content in his spiritual life because he is not trying to be other than he is, to be bigger than he really is. This is a lullaby of the spirit.

If you have ever had the chance to play hide and seek in a big house you will have realized that being small gives you more possibilities.

The smaller we are, the more places we fit into. That rings true in many everyday contexts. If we are undemanding or do not have high expectations for ourselves, we are more likely to be able to value the little we have, to be flexible about what faces us. We value the simple things in life and are not perpetually disappointed. The Psalmist depicts the contentment which goes with not asking for anything, being peaceful in simple homely things. This domestic simplicity is beautiful.

That is what waiting upon the Lord (verse 3) is about: not trying to play God but letting ourselves depend on him; realizing that we don't bring anything into the world, and we don't take anything out. Nothing that we have is because of us, it's because of God.

The Psalmist wants us to begin with God. So does St Bernard. This basic dependence, complete humility, is the foundation of a spiritual life where we put not ourselves but God at the centre. This utter simplicity is freeing and gives deep joy. We're not always failing to live up to our own expectations, the world is not always failing to satisfy us, because we know both we and the world around us are insufficient. Only God can truly satisfy us. Once we figure that out, we chase less often after other things, we're less disappointed in life, and the whole stressful list of things to do becomes less important to us. We realize not only that we are small, but also that our plans and projects are pretty small too.

We've returned to our initial Lenten thoughts about being small and humble, and consequently being in a good place to learn. Tomorrow is the beginning of Passiontide; the tone of our Lenten journey is altering. We've been through difficult times and more refreshing thoughts, accepting that they're usually all mixed up together. Now we're preparing for the most intense two weeks of Lent. Now, therefore, is a good point to pause and look back over where we've got to so far. What new Songs of the Spirit have we learnt? As we have been gazing upon God, how has his gaze upon us changed us? What is our prayer for the journey ahead?

*What baggage would you like to put down to make your journey simpler?*

# WEEK 5: PASSIONTIDE

From place to place

# Monday
## Jerusalem pilgrims

---

## Psalm 122

1  A song of ascents. Of David. I was delighted when they said to
   me, 'Let's go to the house of the Lord.'
2  Our feet stood inside your gates, O Jerusalem;
3  Jerusalem, built up as a city, has been carefully bound together.
4  There the peoples go up, the peoples of the Lord, the duty of
   Israel, to give praise to the name of the Lord.
5  Because it was there that stood the thrones for judgement,
   the thrones of the house of David.
6  Pray for peace for Jerusalem! May those who love her be at
   peace.
7  May there be peace within your fortified city wall, peacefulness
   within your citadels.
8  For the sake of my brothers and my friends, let me say now,
   'Peace be with you.'
9  For the sake of the house of the Lord our God, let me seek
   what is good for you.

We've arrived at Passiontide, the last two weeks of Lent. If you go to
a church where they use decorations to match the different seasons
of the Church year, then you may see the colours change from purple
(or sackcloth) to red. That's because the story has got more intense:
it's not just about repentance and awareness of our need for God.
Things get bloody in the coming days.

This marks a turning point, a new start for us in Lent. Our readings from the Psalms reflect this. First, the tone has changed – we

are concentrating on the journey now. We're not thinking so much about the world around us, its joys and its pains and our place within it, but about where we're heading. Second, there really is a sense in Psalm 122 that we're just starting out.

We start afresh every day: that's possible because of God and his forgiveness of us. Every day is a new day, a second, third or thousandth chance to get close to God. Each day we can remake our choices, every day we can remake the decisions of our baptism to turn to God afresh. The same goes for any important vow we have taken, like a wedding vow. When we got married, I walked up the long aisle of Coventry Cathedral to the words of this psalm, set to music by Hubert Parry. Psalm 122 therefore speaks to me of that new start, the journey with my husband that I commit to every day and every hour.

Psalm 122 begins with setting out on a journey. We hear the excitement of the Psalmist in the first verse, like a child singing, 'We're all going on a summer holiday!' Someone has suggested the trip of a lifetime. The preparations have started. That's something to be overjoyed about.

This trip of a lifetime is to the Temple in Jerusalem. Can you imagine getting so excited about going to a great church or cathedral – St Paul's, or Canterbury Cathedral, or the Vatican? I know some children who would much rather visit the cinema than a church when they're on holiday, and many of us are probably a bit like that sometimes. We don't get quite as excited as we might at the prospect of visiting a great, beautiful, historic church which has seen centuries of prayer. Perhaps we too easily take our many churches for granted.

The Psalmist is getting at more than that. This isn't just a National Trust property with some interesting works of religious art. The Temple in Jerusalem was where God dwelt. It was seen as his very home. That's what makes it the best trip ever – the journey towards God, his presence and his most amazing holiness.

The Psalmist describes preparing for his journey (verse 1), arriving at the gates of Jerusalem (verse 2), and being in awe and wonder at the city as a whole (verse 3). Then he stands aside watching the other pilgrims go by (verse 4), thinking about the very last stage of the journey, the walk through Jerusalem to the Temple, next to which the royal palace of King David stood (verse 5). Royalty and justice were bound together in one place, where both the earthly and the divine King lived.

Let's not forget that this was the journey Jesus was making, about a week before his death. For him too this was a pilgrimage: to the centre of his people's faith, and to the place where he would be proclaimed King and restore justice through his crucifixion and resurrection.

The Temple was a national treasure of the people's heritage. The Psalmist's admiration for the city is described in words that resonate with the Hebrews' former nomadic world. A wandering people, they pitched tents throughout their journey; one way of reading the Hebrew word to describe the city of Jerusalem, 'carefully bound together', relates to the language used for putting up a tent: binding the canvas together. Tents were important in Jewish history: the Ark of the Covenant, the very first home made for God, was portable (Exodus 25). The journeying people of God carried around their holy things, including the tablets of the Ten Commandments. This Ark of the Covenant was a tabernacle, a large and intricately decorated trunk designed to carry the emblems of the presence of God with them on their journey through the wilderness.

Tents, tabernacles, the Temple: this pilgrimage is a holy journey with the presence of God as the end point. There's something else too: the idea of the peoples 'going up' is precisely that used throughout the headings of this series of psalms 'of ascents'. They 'go up' to give praise to God.

'Going up': we talk about 'going up' to big cities or important places, even to university. Or it could be about our growth and development, 'going up to senior school' or 'going up in the world'. What about pilgrims 'going up'? It is like the angels of God ascending and descending on Jacob's ladder in Genesis, or incense symbolizing the ascent of the prayers of the faithful to heaven, or even Jesus himself ascending into heaven. Ascending is heavenly. We do it spiritually every time we 'lift up our hearts'.

The last four verses of the psalm are heartfelt prayers for peace – peace in Jerusalem, peace for the people of Jerusalem. The Psalmist knows he has a duty to pray for this centre of his faith and his history, for his brothers and sisters. The prayers come flooding out of him. As the pilgrim has ascended to contemplate God's presence, so he finds himself praying intently, lovingly, for this holy place and everyone he shares it with.

'Going up' to contemplate God, we can pray that we will be filled with such love, such peace, that we want it for everyone. Perhaps that is what makes places truly holy.

*Where in the world would you most like to visit, and why?*

# Tuesday

## Pilgrims through time

———•◆•———

## Psalm 90

1 A prayer of Moses, man of God.
   O Lord, you have been a refuge for us in generation after
   generation.
2 Before the mountains were born, and you gave birth to the
   earth and the world, from eternity to eternity you are God.
3 You make mankind return again to dust, and you say, 'Return
   to the adamant, you sons of Adam!'
4 For a thousand years in your eyes are as yesterday which has
   just gone by, or like a few hours within the night.
5 You drown men in sleep; they become in the morning like the
   grass that has grown afresh.
6 At dawn it flourishes afresh; in the evening it is withered and
   dried up.
7 For we are finished off by your anger, and by your rage are we
   utterly dismayed.
8 You have set our guilt right in front of us, your very presence
   has shone a floodlight on our secrets.
9 For all our days pass away in your wrath, our years are finished
   off like a sigh.
10 The span of our life is seventy years, or if we are strong, eighty
   years; but even the prime of our lives is trouble and sorrow,
   because even that passes away quickly and we fly off.
11 Who really knows the strength of your anger? Your wrath is as
   great as the fear you inspire.

12 Teach us to count our days honestly, so that we may grow wisdom in our heart.
13 Turn, O Lᴏʀᴅ! How long? Have some compassion for your servants!
14 Satisfy us at daybreak with your steadfast love, so that we may shout with joy and be happy all our days.
15 Make us happy for as long as the days that you have brought us low, for as long as the years that we have seen trouble.
16 Let us your servants see your miracles, and our children see your glory.
17 May the kindness of the Lord our God be upon us, and may the work of our hands be successful; indeed, may the work of our hands be successful!

Yesterday the theme was 'going up', setting out towards our destination in God. Today in Psalm 90 this is turned in on itself. Now the prayer is about returning, being well past our prime, on the last leg of our life's journey.

This psalm is called 'A Prayer'. This appears as a heading to only four other psalms; yet it is the word with which Psalm 72 closes Book 2 of the Psalter: 'the end of the prayers of David the son of Jesse'. We've already spotted that not all of the Psalms are actually addressed to God, and some are calls to prayer and praise. So what is it that makes a prayer a prayer?

The Hebrew word translated 'prayer' here, *tephillah*, might come from the Hebrew verbal root meaning 'to judge'. Perhaps the pray-er is calling on God to act as judge. Usually a text called a *tephillah* is a complaint addressed to God. There are other suggested explanations too, though. One such is that *tephillah* might mean 'to judge oneself'; that is, to examine oneself, to be penitent, contrite.

How penitent are we when we pray? It goes back to our awareness of our need for God. We can't be in a good relationship with God by our own efforts because there's so much we are lacking. Do we want to judge ourselves? Do we want God to judge us?

In Psalm 90 God is both wrathful judge and refuge. It is fascinating to stop and notice how fast the Psalmist moves from thinking about God as 'our refuge' (verse 1), via reflection on God's greatness as opposed to humanity's fleeting transience (verses 2–7), to verse upon verse dwelling on God as judge. This judge's presence is so bright that he is like a floodlight which shows everything up clearly even in the dark (verse 8).

This is a pretty terrifying judge. Nothing gets past him, and he can get very angry, says the Psalmist. God's wrath can have terrible consequences, as spelled out in verses 7, 9 and 11. But we can't really avoid this anger, because we can't help but get things wrong; God can't help but notice when we get things wrong; and our getting things wrong makes God cross. Therefore God must be always angry, and we must be always justly punished with suffering. So it's a natural progression of thought that leads to the Psalmist saying to God, as it were: 'Hang on a mo, God! Can you help us here? Please?'

It only takes a moment for God to help us break out of this vicious circle. Even if we had a lifetime we'd never manage it in our own strength. Our lives, muses the Psalmist, whether we reach seventy or eighty years of age at most, are to the eternal God as long as the lifespan of a blade of grass might seem to us.

The Psalmist thinks of himself and his peers as being over the hill in terms of age and years (verses 9 onwards). He's probably reached the peak of life (verse 10), but that's only felt tiresome and troubled. How much longer will life last? And how much longer must he endure these years of suffering and distress (verses 12–13)? Isn't it about time things started looking up (verses 13–17)? Can't we have some good times still before we die?

We can imagine Jesus thinking the same in the Garden of Gethsemane, which we'll concentrate on in just over a week. 'Can't you take this cup from me?' he prays to God.

We will all die. Our return to the earth is inevitable. One day our bones or the ashes of our bodies will be laid to rest in the ground. Psalm 90 points to the symmetry of birth and death in verses 2–3. The translation I've given of verse 3 makes a little more of the sound of the words than the Hebrew does in this instance: the reference to man as the 'son of Adam' is a reminder of the second creation story in Genesis, where man or Adam is made literally from the 'adamant', from the earth. Our death is a return to the atoms and molecules that make up our bodies. We will actually be pushing up the daisies as our dead bodies in turn enrich the earth in which we will lie. There is also an echo of the 'son of man' language we saw in Psalm 8, with its regard for creation.

As Christians, we know that this isn't the end of the story. We may not know precisely, clearly, what happens next, but we know that our bodily death is but a beginning. It is only at our bodily death that we can really, truly hope for complete union with God, for new life, with new bodies which will entirely suit the heavenly existence to which we are called.

Psalm 90 is often used on Remembrance Sunday as churches think about those who have given up their lives fighting for their countries. There is certainly a sense of morbidity about many of these verses, but a sense of majesty too. All this is in the hand of God. Perhaps this is how God is our refuge in its very truest sense: our refuge, our dwelling place, our habitation, our home. We return home after a journey. After the journey of life, we return to our God. Our journey out is directed towards God. So is the return. Only when we return will we stop asking 'Is there still time?' or 'How much longer?'

Then we will finally know satisfaction, we will no longer yearn for something more. Only God can satisfy us. We can only satisfy God with Jesus' help. As we prepare for the final days of the Passion, we wonder again at Jesus who alone could break humanity out of that vicious circle of sin and suffering from which Psalm 90 prays for escape.

*If you could fulfil one hope in this life, what would it be?*

# Wednesday
## Waiting pilgrims

———◆•◆———

## Psalm 27

1   Of David. The LORD is my light and my salvation, so who is
    there for me to be afraid of? The LORD is the fortress of my life,
    so who is there for me to dread?
2   When wicked people come up to me to destroy my body, my
    enemies and those who are hostile to me, it is they who end
    up stumbling and falling, not me!
3   Even if an army were to range themselves against me, my heart
    would not be afraid; if a battle were to start against me, even
    in these circumstances would I have confidence.
4   One thing I ask of the LORD, only this do I seek: to live in the
    house of the LORD all the days of my life, to look upon the
    beauty of the LORD, and to contemplate in his Temple.
5   For he will hide me in his shelter in the day of trouble, he will
    conceal me in a secret place in his own home, he will raise me
    up high on inaccessible rock.
6   And now, indeed my head is high above my enemies who
    surround me! So let me make sacrifices in his Temple, shouting
    for joy, let me sing and let me make music to the LORD!
7   Hear my voice, O LORD, when I call out, be kind to me, and
    answer me!
8   I hear your words in my heart, 'Seek my presence!' So I shall
    seek your presence, O LORD.
9   Do not hide your presence from me, do not turn from your
    servant in anger! You are my helper! Do not leave me! Do not
    desert me, O God of my salvation!

10   Even if my father and my mother desert me, the Lᴏʀᴅ would gather me to himself.
11   Teach me your way, O Lᴏʀᴅ, and guide me on a level path, to avoid my watchful foes.
12   Do not hand me over to the desire of my enemies, for lying witnesses have stood up against me, breathing out violence.
13   Were it not for my belief that I would see the goodness of the Lᴏʀᴅ in the land of the living . . .
14   Wait for the Lᴏʀᴅ! Be strong and take heart! Wait for the Lᴏʀᴅ!

Our life's journey is a pilgrimage. The Psalmist in Psalms 122 and 90 makes an invitation: set your face towards God, and return to God.

Sharing the gaze of God: as we set our faces towards God so God sets his face towards us. The language of 'setting the face' sounds archaic; it's a typically Hebrew expression. Hebrew is a very physical language. It describes God in bodily terms, which is astonishing when you think about it. It is effectively inviting the incarnation, looking forward to God being embodied in Jesus Christ. God's power and might is described as his 'hand' or his 'right hand'. And his gaze, loving or angry, is expressed as his 'eyes'. His very presence is often related to his 'face'. So when God turns his face away, he removes himself from our presence. And when we seek the presence of God, we are even hoping to meet him face to face.

This idea makes up a large part of Psalm 27. I like this psalm because from it comes the motto of the University of Oxford: 'The Lord is my light and my salvation' (verse 1). Being in the presence of God is like being in the light. Yesterday's divine floodlight showing up all our flaws was fearful. But light is truly wonderful. Where would we be without it? It's something that gives life, that makes things clear, that helps us to see, to understand. It helps us in our journeying.

We journey in the light, and we journey towards the light. That is our salvation. Salvation surrounds us and salvation is our destination. God is both our navigator and the destination we're heading for.

God in Psalm 27 is depicted both as the person who saves, as the act of saving in itself, and as the salvation or the eternal safety where we land up. His saving power gives the Psalmist staggering confidence (verses 1–3), and this saving power is God's very presence (verses 4–6). No wonder the Psalmist always wants to be close to God, close to salvation.

He doesn't just mean being close though: he means being within God's own home, which is a way to describe the Temple, or the sanctuary on the 'Temple Rock' at the summit of the mount in Jerusalem. This adds another layer of significance, a physical symbolism, to the image of God our rock. The high tor idealized in other psalms as a retreat, a stronghold, is like the rocky crag on which the Temple was built. Verses 4–6 express profound longing for life in the Temple: not just as the goal of the pilgrimage, but as the place to stay for ever. In verse 9 the Psalmist refers to himself as the servant of God (a term commonly found in the Hebrew Bible). Many servants of God in the Temple would have had worship responsibilities. Certainly in verse 6 the Psalmist pictures himself there, praising God loudly and unstoppably.

But who's listening? He is in the presence of God, yes, but also in the presence of the Psalmist's enemies (verse 6), and he begins to worry that God isn't in fact present (verse 9). Fortunately this wavering doubt doesn't last for too long, yet it points out how each prayer we speak aloud is a testimony to what we believe. Whatever we say to God may be said in the presence of other people who can hear what we're saying. The Psalmist sometimes uses this as a way of threatening his enemies by his own great confidence in God. He's saying clearly in front of his enemies, 'God's on *my* side, so watch out!'

The other very real point here is that however great our faith, it's normal for it sometimes to wobble. Life's a mixture of wonderful moments when belief in a good God is easy, and difficult moments when we scratch our heads and say, 'But where is God now?' That very real mixture of life experiences is one reason that I've chosen the psalms I have so far – they're a mixed bag. The Psalms provide a fabulous range of things to think about. They reflect an immense amount of life. Should we be miserable in Lent and cheerful at Easter? It's not so simple: that's not how the world works. At least, not yet. The kingdom of God is both already here and not yet here.

Psalms often have both good moments and bad moments. Confident streaks and doubtful shadows. Light and dark. Despite his gallant confidence, the Psalmist is clearly feeling threatened in Psalm 27. This whole psalm is a meditation building up his self-confidence.

The psalm closes with words used more recently as a well-known Taizé chant. For all the passion entailed in seeking God's presence, for all our eagerness to come to God, what we finally end up with is stillness. We look towards, journey towards, seek the presence of our God; but God will always seek us. His salvation is seeking us out. So at the last, we need to wait for God. This is a journey which requires us to be still.

*What places have most shaped you?*

# Thursday

## *Home from home*

---·•·---

## Psalm 132

¹ A song of ascents. Remember, O Lᴏʀᴅ, for David, all the difficulties he faced,

² how he made a vow to the Lᴏʀᴅ and a promise to the Mighty One of Jacob:

³ 'I shall not go into my home, I shall not get into bed,

⁴ I shall not give sleep to my eyes, to my eyelids I shall give no rest,

⁵ until I find a place for the Lᴏʀᴅ, a building for the Mighty One of Jacob.'

⁶ Yes! we heard about it in Ephrathah, we found it in the land of Jaar.

⁷ Let us then go to his habitation, let us bow ourselves low by his footstool!

⁸ Rise up, O Lᴏʀᴅ, to your resting place, you, and the Ark where your strength resides!

⁹ Let your priests clothe themselves with rightness, let your faithful followers shout out in joy!

¹⁰ For the sake of David, your servant, do not turn away your face from your anointed one!

¹¹ The Lᴏʀᴅ made a vow to David, a true oath that he will not go back on: 'One of your own offspring I shall set on your throne,

¹² if your sons keep my covenant and my instructions which I shall teach them. Even their sons, for ever and ever, shall sit on your throne.'

¹³ For the Lᴏʀᴅ has chosen Zion, he has desired her for his dwelling place.

14 'This is my resting place for ever and ever, here will I live,
because I have desired it.

15 I shall truly bless Zion's food supply, her poor I will satisfy with
bread.

16 I will clothe Zion's priests with salvation, and her faithful
people will shout, shout with joy!

17 There I shall make a horn grow for David, I have set up a
sanctuary lamp for my anointed one.

18 His enemies I shall clothe with shame, while on him shall his
crown sparkle!'

The homely themes of the psalms of ascents begin Psalm 132. David thinks of his own home, even his bed (verse 3), and realizes that the Ark, the symbol of God's presence, does not have such a place.

This psalm is about holy places and holy vows. David has a sumptuous palace to live in, while God has no such place. The contrast is quickly established. So David vows that he will not rest until he finds a place God can call home. That seems like a pretty daft vow – building a Temple would take years. Is David really planning not to go home or to sleep for that length of time? He wouldn't survive. If he's anything like the rest of us, sleep deprivation would quickly have an impact on his decision-making and kingly work.

Is David making a vow he knows he'll never keep? What else is going on here?

David grew up during the wars with the Philistines – wars which featured Samson, Goliath, and all sorts of stories of heroes and battles. The book of 1 Samuel charts some of these. The Philistines captured the Ark of the Covenant, but while they had it in their possession, they were terrified by its power, so they loaded it on a driverless cart and it made its own way out of Philistine territory. It reached Beth-Shemesh, where the people recognized it and rejoiced.

Psalm 132 refers to how David went to fetch the Ark from Ephrathah, where it had been kept after the Philistines released it. Mention of the Ark itself only comes in verse 8. Verses 7–9 are an encouragement to the Psalmist's fellow worshippers to make that journey to God's presence.

God doesn't need anyone to find a place for him or make a home for him, because he has always gone in front of his people. Unlike the idols of the neighbouring peoples, the God of the Hebrews can make his own way, take up his own place. That fact is conveyed particularly in verses 11–18, the rest of the psalm, where God makes a vow which goes way beyond David's promises in the first half.

Thrones signify the fixed point of a kingdom. This is the centre of the kingdom, the place where the king sits. David has his throne, and he wants God to be similarly enthroned. But God replies with a vow that points to David's children, his sons and their sons (verses 11–12). If they stay in close relationship with God, then God will enthrone them generation by generation. God transcends David's attempts to enthrone God, and looks instead to enthroning David's son Solomon.

Solomon built the First Temple in Jerusalem (the Second Temple was built on the Jewish return from exile in Babylon, and was destroyed in AD 70). So David's vow not to sleep until he had made a home for God clearly was not literally fulfilled by David himself.

In fact it had already been fulfilled by God. As verse 13 tells us, God has already chosen Jerusalem as his dwelling place, his home. What is it for God to make his home somewhere? God's *decision* that he belongs there is what actually makes that place his home.

Significantly, the Ark, the sign of God's presence, was portable. God is not confined by human intentions. God did not need David to build him a Temple; Solomon's construction of the Temple (where so many of the psalms would eventually be sung) was above all a sign of his own devotion to God and the covenant.

Naturally God blesses such commitment, promising first food for his people (verse 15), and second the beauty of holiness. Verse 16 pictures the priests and the congregation: whatever your tradition, imagine an inspiring act of worship, the building packed with faithful throngs. Verse 17 is about the Temple fittings. The 'horn' could either be a sign of plenty, which would tie in with verse 15, or a reference to the shape of the altar (many Old Testament references to the altar in the Temple describe it as having 'horns', best envisaged as very ornate corners resembling bulls' horns).

Psalm 132 is easily understood as a 'pilgrimage psalm'. It invites movement at every turn. The Ark is making a journey, from captivity to Jerusalem: God's presence is a journeying presence. David cannot settle until he is confident that God is present among his people. Thrones made by human hands cannot hold God still; God chooses the places he will bless by his presence. Yet where a place is chosen that is clearly blessed by God, that place in turn invites God's people to journey towards it, towards sanctuary.

This provides us today with encouragement to start afresh our journey towards God – whether through a physical pilgrimage or a spiritual one. Moving towards God is also about being still, an idea we explored yesterday. Moving towards God can be about moving inwards within ourselves, our hearts and minds; or about moving outwards, looking beyond ourselves and responding to God's invitation to us to transcend our earthly lives.

It can also be about opening ourselves up to God to come closer to us, to make his home in us. In Psalm 132, God has decided he has a home on earth long before, as Christians proclaim, he made his home in the womb of Mary prior to Jesus' incarnation. In some Christian traditions, the Virgin Mary is seen as the Ark of the New Covenant. God promises a sanctuary lamp shining in the Temple for his anointed (verse 17). Could this anointed one be not only David or Solomon, but Christ, who is literally the Anointed One?

Our own anointing shines out at baptism as we make our home within God's people. God has already decided on us to be his home. Let's be at home with him.

*Think how you might create a holy space for God in your home. What would it be like?*

# Friday

## *Who can be a pilgrim?*

---

**Psalm 24**

1   Of David. A psalm. To the LORD belong the earth, and all the
    fullness of the world, and everyone who lives in it!
2   For it is he who gave it a foundation on the seas, and on the
    rivers established it.
3   Who shall go up to the mount of the LORD, and who shall rise
    up in his holy place?
4   The one who has clean hands, and a pure heart, and does
    not lift up his soul to worthless things, and does not swear
    deceitfully.
5   He shall carry away a blessing from the LORD, and rightness
    from God his salvation.
6   This is the generation who seek him, the descendants of Jacob,
    who come to see your face. *Selah.*
7   O gates, lift up your heads! Be lifted up, you everlasting
    entrances, and may the King of glory come in!
8   Who is this King of glory? The LORD who has power and
    strength, the LORD who has strength in battle.
9   O gates, lift up your heads! Lift them up, you everlasting
    entrances, and may the King of glory come in!
10  Who is he, this King of glory? The LORD who has armies of
    people behind him, he is the King of glory! *Selah.*

We care more than we admit about 'who's in' and 'who's out': sports
teams, TV shows, shortlists, selective schools – it matters to us. If we're
'in', the membership of a group defines us; if we're 'out' we wonder

what we're missing, or why we were deselected. It puts boundaries in place, borders that we may never have the chance to cross again.

Being excluded brings bitterness. It implies judgement on us. The desire to belong is strong. To whom or what do you want to belong? Do you give thanks if you do belong somewhere? And how does not belonging affect you? Being excluded can be a lonely and desolate experience.

We exclude people too, from conversations or committees. When we do so, we may be causing others hurt. Sometimes it is unavoidable, sometimes unconscious. But if we can be aware of it, remembering what it feels like to be excluded, we might grow into richer human beings because of it.

Finances exclude. Politics excludes. Faiths exclude.

Does God exclude? Psalm 24 is sometimes called an 'entrance' liturgy, to accompany the pilgrim's arrival at the gates of the Temple, as he seeks entry into the house and presence of God. Look how it's built up: from the widest expanses of the earth, the fullness of the world (verse 1), to the seas and rivers (verse 2), to the one and only holy mountain (verse 3). There's a kind of 'funnelling' effect as the Temple Mount comes into focus at the centre of this contemplation. We stand at the foot of the Temple Mount, preparing to go up.

Who can go up? That's the question of this psalm. Who's allowed in?

Verse 4 gives the answer: it is the person who upholds God's Torah, his instruction. Some think this psalm is within another mini-collection, Psalms 15–24. Psalm 24 is placed in relationship to Psalms 15 and 19, which are about being upright and keeping the Torah. This means that the Torah features at the beginning, middle and end of this sub-collection. The Torah is viewed as the key to entry into God's presence.

Who then can get close to God? In Passiontide the themes of Lent are intensified. The time set aside for our penitence is now well past. In a couple of days it will be Holy Week. Have we been keeping our Lenten disciplines? Have we been achieving a closer union with God? Have we been diligent in prayer and fasting?

My guess is that we've all had bad days this far into Lent: days when we've failed to live up to our own expectations, or our church's expectations. Is there a risk that we don't live up to the Psalmist's standards, that we 'aren't good enough', that we've let other people, ourselves, and God down, at a time when we should have been trying even harder than usual?

We stand at the threshold of Holy Week and hope we might be admitted; now we've come this far, to the foot of the mountain, we wonder if we'll be allowed to approach yet closer to our holy God. But there is tension here. Verse 4 asks a lot of us. We're not perfect, and it seems to require that we should be.

So do we turn back, disconsolate, disappointed? No. We're not the only ones seeking God. There are many of us: a whole generation at any one time (verse 6). The righteous exemplar is but one person. Surely we're not all going to be turned away?

The triumphant, repetitive call of the Psalmist to the gates of the Temple banishes our fears (verses 7 and 9). Fling wide the gates! All is opened up, access is granted.

Now the focus shifts. Suddenly it's no longer on the morally perfect person. Instead it's on the King of glory. It's not about who is the individual righteous person. It's about who is the 'King of glory' (verses 8 and 10). The question is asked and answered twice. It makes the point. This isn't about a faultless earthly king. This is about the Lord, about God.

Who's entering the Temple? God. God – and he's leading the way for us all. He's not on the other side of the gates. He's on *the same side as us*. He's getting us in.

Contrary to what gates make us think of, there's no exclusion here. God has whole hosts of people behind him (verse 10). He's pictured as a mighty Lord leading great valiant armies into battle, armies of people who will not be beaten.

The entrance ritual pictures us drawn in *to* God's presence *by* God.

Accessibility is important in society. We need to make sure our buildings have wheelchair access, that all people have access to services and opportunities, that we don't just do things for a minority but make them available to as many as possible at once. It's not always easy. But this isn't about one or two campaign groups leading the way. This is about God helping us progress. Making accessibility accessible, as it were.

Neither is this just a one-off. Verses 7 and 9 describe the 'everlasting entrances'. This path is open for all time. Opened at the approach of the King of glory, they remain open for all who gather behind him.

That means us. We may not have had the most successful Lent; or we may have had the most holy Lent we've ever experienced. Wherever we are right now, we know that as we journey towards the foot of the mountain, the possibility of pilgrimage is there for us all. Our ability to approach God grows as we practise it, falteringly or confidently.

It's not so different from the way of the cross. Jesus goes before, opening the way of life, the gates to God's kingdom. We gather as hosts of people behind this mighty Lord, the King of glory. God becomes accessible to all, for all.

*To what groups do you belong, or want to belong, and why?*

# Saturday

## Pilgrimage into the presence of God

———•◦•———

## Psalm 100

¹ A psalm for thanksgiving. Raise a shout to the Lᴏʀᴅ, all the earth!

² be servants to the Lᴏʀᴅ with joy, come to him with a glad sound!

³ Know this, that the Lᴏʀᴅ, he is God. He has made us, we belong to him, we are his people, and the flock under his shepherding care.

⁴ Enter his gates with thanksgiving, his courtyards with songs of praise! Praise him! Bless his name!

⁵ For the Lᴏʀᴅ is good; his love lasts for ever; and his faithfulness is for every generation.

Thanksgiving. What a gift.

Over 30 psalms in the Psalter could be classified as 'thanksgiving psalms'. Oddly, though, Psalm 100 is the only one that has 'thanksgiving' in the heading like this (although there are plenty of references to thanksgiving songs elsewhere). Thanksgiving, praise and hymns are closely related.

'All people that on earth do dwell', or 'Old Hundredth', is a well-known English hymn. It's good for a grand occasion or a hearty sing. Hymns and songs are a great way to worship. Indeed, Jesus himself sang in his worship. The Passion narratives in Matthew and Mark refer to Jesus and his disciples singing during the Passover supper. The traditional psalms for singing at this Jewish festival meal are Psalms 113–118. That's why we will be looking at this sequence of psalms next week.

Tomorrow is Palm Sunday. I'm often at Hilfield Friary on Palm Sunday with a lovely bunch of university students. Just before the Eucharist we gather on the top field and take up willow branches complete with blossom, our Dorset equivalent of palms. Simple, rustic musical instruments are handed out and we process down the lane to the chapel singing our hosannas. We're told to 'Go forth and make noise!', which is a worship instruction the undergraduates particularly enjoy.

Being rightly noisy in worship can be liberating, expressive, fun. Of course the most buoyant noise-making will happen in a week's time, at our Easter services, if we dare look ahead to that as Holy Week draws close. What better way to celebrate the resurrection than with shouts and laughter and unstoppable outbursts of joy?

One of the reasons we don't count Sundays within the days of Lent is because every Sunday is a celebration of the resurrection. We are usually toned down during Lent, of course; it's a subdued season and there's a wider context. But every time we come together, we are doing a whole host of things in our praise and prayer. Think about the word 'confession'. We confess our sins, yes; we also confess our faith. Confession is both a pouring out of our own penitence, and a bold restatement of the gospel and our salvation story. So if I think I shouldn't be talking about the resurrection right now – before we really celebrate Easter – well, this is why I am doing so. We just can't hold it back . . . and all our days include mixed blessings of joy and sorrow. To ignore one entirely and focus solely on the other cannot wholly do justice to our real lived experiences. Life isn't simple. There is always good reason – if we can get in touch with it – to sing, to praise, to give thanks.

The Eucharist is, for me and for many Christians, a crucial way to witness to Jesus' story, important for our own spiritual nourishment. The Eucharist is a developed form of thanksgiving. Based on Jesus' commandment to his disciples at the Last Supper, which we'll particularly be thinking about next Thursday, the actions of taking the bread and wine and sharing them make Jesus present for us each time in a host of ways. Eating and drinking together, we remember Christ's presence among us, the mystery and wonder of God made flesh, the awesome Holy Week and Easter story of crucifixion and resurrection.

I hope that you have experienced or will encounter awesome moments in your journeys in Christ. What can be more special than the possibility time and again of coming into God's presence, and of Christ making himself present among us? That is one of the deep joys of the Eucharist, something for which we rightly give thanks. And in giving thanks, we even find ourselves receiving.

How do we prepare for such breathtaking spiritual moments? Sometimes they will take us by surprise. But when our spiritual nourishment is a part of our regular daily or weekly worship, we can take time to try and ready ourselves for an especially focused encounter with God.

We are, after all, God's servants (verse 2). We each serve God in many different ways, from engaging in private prayer to leading worship, from learning about him to letting the love we receive from him shape our lives and actions. Serving is about humility once again. To serve is not to take up the elevated place of the important person, but to get down on our knees. To be a servant is to approach our master with respect and reverence. After all, we belong to him (verse 3) – not the other way round.

Steadying ourselves for thanksgiving involves gathering ourselves, both as individuals and as a community, in order to bring together before God all that we are – all that we have been this week, all that we hope to be next week – and to present ourselves before God in humble truth. That again points to the two sides of confession: our own lack, and God's great plenty. Taking time to reflect on God before an act of worship helps us prepare ourselves to meet with him. And practising meeting with God in our daily earthly lives is the best preparation we can make for our eventual meeting with God beyond this life.

Psalm 100 charts this kind of preparation for worship and thanksgiving. It's hard to tell where preparation finishes and thanksgiving starts, because all of our lives can be infused with thanksgiving. Today, before we head in word or deed into the Palm Sunday processions, is a good time to stop and think about how we come into church, how we settle ourselves down ready for worship. Do we chatter excitedly, fall straight into silent prayer, or join in the songs that are being sung at the front? There are no rights and wrongs, but our entry into thanksgiving is a conscious act in itself.

As we enter into Holy Week, it's no bad thing to think about how we simply enter into the holy.

*'Jesus, our Immanuel!': the Hebrew name 'Immanuel' literally means 'God-With-Us'. What does 'God-With-Us' mean to you?*

# WEEK 6: HOLY WEEK

## To a holy place

# Monday

—•◆•—

## Psalm 113

1 Hallelujah! Praise, O servants of the LORD, praise the name of the LORD!
2 Let the name of the LORD be blessed from now unto eternity!
3 From the rising of the sun to its setting, the LORD's name be praised!
4 High up over all the nations is the LORD; over the heavens is his glory!
5 Who is like the LORD our God? He who takes the highest seat,
6 he who makes himself low even to see into the heavens, and into the earth,
7 he who raises up from the dust the poor man, from the rubbish heap lifts the desperate scavenger,
8 to make them take their places with great men, with the nobility of the nation,
9 he who makes the childless woman of the household take her place as a joyful mother of sons? Hallelujah!

After Palm Sunday we look towards the Triduum, the three holy days from the evening of Maundy Thursday. We know they're on the horizon, that we don't have much time left in Jesus' story. This is the last week of Jesus' life. He has made his journey up to the holy city of Jerusalem for the coming Passover festival. He has hinted again and again that it's in Jerusalem, he knows, that he will meet his death. His death is intimately tied up with this great festival.

The Passover is the Jewish celebration of the Israelites' escape from slavery in Egypt. It involves a stylized re-enactment and retelling of their last dinner in Egypt. God sent the so-called ten plagues upon Egypt to persuade Pharaoh to let the Israelites go. The only one that really got to Pharaoh was the night when the Egyptians' firstborn, both people and animals, died. The Israelites obediently sacrificed lambs and smeared the blood on their doorposts to protect their own households from this danger. They had a special meal, which was about having something to eat in preparation for making a move to freedom.

Throughout the Passover meal, Psalms 113–118 are sung in order. They are called the 'Hallel psalms', because 'Hallelujah' is often repeated at the beginning and end. 'Hallel' means 'praise', and 'Jah' is the name of God (the first part of 'Jahweh', a variant of 'Yahweh'). So 'Hallelujah' means 'Praise the Lord!' In different versions of these texts, the Hallelujahs occur in different places – for instance, the Hallelujah in verse 9 here is sometimes read as the beginning of Psalm 114 rather than the end of Psalm 113. That points to the way these psalms in Jewish liturgy through ages past were read as a block, a collection truly belonging together.

These are clearly celebratory psalms – so why read them in Holy Week as the story gets darker and darker? Many Christians stop saying 'Hallelujah' (or 'Alleluia') during Lent. But even in his darkest days and hours, Jesus was singing these psalms. It's been a theme this Lent: the mixture of light and dark, joy and pain. Holy Week is no different.

Psalm 113 celebrates the power of God. Praying like this can lift our spirits. Simple verses like 'your deeds are marvels, and my soul knows that intimately' (Psalm 139.14) are great reminders to us that God works miracles. They are a constant affirmation of our faith even when lament feels more fitting to our mood.

It's the same here. The praise is strong, hard-hitting. The 'Hallel' word is repeated, and God and his name are used interchangeably. The psalms used so far in our Lenten meditations have often referred to the names of God, and we've thought about how they are used in relationship to who God is. What's clear in so many places is not just what the different names of God mean, but what the name of God stands for and how powerful it is. God's name is so holy that just the name alone can represent God and work marvels. Sometimes in prayer in our churches today we might repeat the name 'Jesus' for the same reason – evoking God, we can open ourselves and our world to miraculous deeds of power. As in the hymn 'At the name of Jesus / Ev'ry knee shall bow', the name of God is itself to be worshipped and adored.

God's praiseworthiness is described by picturing how high up he is. We talk of being 'high up' in management, or sitting at 'the top table'. God is higher than the highest thing we can imagine: the Psalmist looks up to him as higher even than the heavens (verse 4).

This is what's most spectacular. Although God is so high up, he 'makes himself low to see even into the heavens and into the earth'. Bending low paradoxically makes him even higher, more worthy of praise. As he sees in, so he acts in the heavens and the earth, especially in the lowest parts of the earth – the rubbish tips, the desperate human lives.

The story of the Incarnation at Christmas celebrates just this fact, that God in Jesus chose to make himself lowly and poured himself out in the humblest setting possible, in the humblest guise he could. As Christ, God truly makes himself so low as to see even into the deepest, darkest corners of the earth.

On the cross, Jesus is raised up. He will be exalted on Calvary as an improbable king, but those who wanted Jesus dead will find their mockery of him turned upside down in his resurrection. Being high and low are transposed and muddled up; they are made level.

That's what we see in God's actions to help the poor and needy in Psalm 113. Lifting up the poor man, the scavenger, the childless woman, he makes them equal to the greatest nobles and to those around them. Who is as great as the Lord our God?

That's right, says the Psalmist: '*Who is like the* Lord *our God?*' The God who from on high cares so much about the lowest of the low that he descends to their level to bring them up from their humble places. God's place is in heaven, but he makes his place on the earth, among humanity, and he takes care to bend down to all levels in order to achieve his miraculous works. There is no one comparable to our God.

The Hebrew name of the great angel called Michael literally means 'Who is like God?' Angels have roles as messengers. St Michael, with the Psalmist of Psalm 113, reminds us to wonder at just how great God is. That's the power of Michael's name. The power of God's name is great enough to be blessed from the rising of the sun to its setting: all day long and from one end of the earth to the other.

Praise the Lord!

*What will you celebrate about God today?*

# Tuesday

———◆———

## Psalm 114

1   When Israel came out from Egypt, the house of Jacob from a
    people of strange speech,
2   Judah became his holy seat, Israel his realm.
3   The sea saw, and fled; the Jordan river went back on itself.
4   The mountains bounced like rams, the hills like the lambs of
    the flock.
5   What was it for you, O sea, that you fled? O Jordan, that you
    went back on yourself?
6   O mountains, that you bounced around like rams? O hills, like
    the lambs of the flock?
7   Face to face with the Lord – tremble, O earth – face to face
    with the God of Jacob,
8   he who turned the rock into a pool of water, the flint stone
    into a fountain of water!

Alongside the Hallel psalms, the Passover meal traditionally involves
a child asking the head of the household what all the rituals mean.
It's a way for every generation to retell the story of the Israelites'
escape from slavery in Egypt to freedom in the promised land.

The Psalmist loads these few verses with memories of Israel's
salvation history. Shared memories tell the story of a community's
identity: their common past, the direction they're travelling in together, their future hopes. As the faithful sing and pray this psalm
together, they remember where they've come from and strengthen
the bonds of their relationships.

Remembering together builds up the community. When we spend time with beloved friends or family, we sometimes ask, 'Do you remember when . . .?' We smile together at a joyful past, or heave a mutual sigh of relief that old painful experiences are long since left behind.

The Israelites have a clear sense of their common roots. Their worship unites them in their shared remembrances. Reminding themselves and one another of God and his love for them, they find solace at times of hardship, and reason for praise at good moments. Calling to mind God's covenant and teaching, they acknowledge their faults and correct their ways. They share their relationship with God with one another.

The Passover and exodus from Egypt is crucial to the salvation story, and central to Jewish self-identity through the generations. At the Passover, the child's questions act out such a remembering of traditions. Psalm 114 is a worshipping performance of this, tightly formed and condensed into a memorable few verses.

It's simply told, as in a response to a child. There are the rhythmic balances: between Israel and Jacob (verse 1), different descriptions of the same people; and again between Judah and Israel (verse 2), united at this stage in their history. Egypt is unimaginable to later generations of youngsters, so the speaker suggests that the peculiar language is Egypt's defining feature (verse 1). The identity marker for Israel on the other hand is a contrasting realm, a kingdom of belonging (verse 2). God's land is more than geographical: it is his people.

Geographical features jump at God's word: the Red Sea is parted (Exodus 14), the River Jordan crossed (Joshua 3), concertina-ing two significant moments in history (verse 3). The quaking mountains and hills (verse 4) echo the cosmic upheavals on Sinai when God gave Moses the Ten Commandments (Exodus 19). Yet this potentially terrifying scene is domesticated to the families of sheep and lambs and their frolicking. The homely tone matches the family context in which such stories are retold.

The repetition highlights this context. Verses 5 and 6 mimic the language of verses 3 and 4 as they question, like a child, why something happened. (Cast your mind to a conversation with a child, when she keeps asking 'why?' It may become wearying but it's an important way to learn, and to teach.) It's almost parrot-fashion, imaginable in a primary school context because it's so formulaic.

These geological features are held responsible for their actions. That they can act at all is surprising when you think about it. Inanimate objects are described as capable of movement, of will, as if they even had some sense of reasoning. It's not that God divides the Red Sea or the River Jordan; it's that the Red Sea parts, the River Jordan changes its course before God. It's not that God shakes the mountains and the hills; it's that they respond to God by trembling.

That's the kind of reasoning that belongs to the sea and river, the mountains and hills. That's why they act as they do. Because God is right there, in their faces. Fleeing and trembling are *natural* ways to respond to God, the awesome Creator as well as the powerful Redeemer.

God as Redeemer is remembered again in the final verse. After the escape from Egypt, during the 40-year exodus journey through the wilderness, the Israelites needed water. At Horeb Moses famously did as God said: he struck a rock and water gushed out. Once again God saved his people.

In order to fit into the pattern of the rest of the psalm, these two kinds of water – the pool and the fountain – must be basic equivalents. They're both there to provide water for drinking. The pool might have been easier for animals to reach, the fountain more accessible for the people. It's interesting that in the passing down of this psalm – a song which is all about the very act of passing down stories and words and texts – the two types of water are set in contrast to each other. Going back to St Jerome in the late fourth century CE, the Latin translation of the Bible, the Vulgate, makes the 'pool' sound like standing water, stagnant water, water you wouldn't want to drink (unlike the 'fountain' of fresh drinking water).

Whether these two kinds of water were meant to be understood as equivalent or different, it's significant that the Psalmist chooses to return to water at the end of the psalm. The Red Sea and the River Jordan both featured early in the psalm; now we read of smaller bodies of water in the final verse. God provides life-giving water, fearsome water; God influences both massive bodies of water and tiny puddles or trickles. Whatever the scale, it's in God's power.

All this is echoed in baptism today. The prayer spoken over the water – whether in a font or a full-immersion pool – refers to the water over which the Holy Spirit moved at creation; the water through which the Israelites travelled at the exodus; and the water in which Jesus himself was baptized by John in the River Jordan. The water of baptism symbolizes a kind of death and rebirth.

Water in Psalm 114 holds together precious nuggets of salvation history which give the Israelites identity. Baptism gives us our true identity and our salvation.

*What stories have given you, or your community, a sense of identity?*

# *Wednesday*

———◆———

## Psalm 115

1 Not to us, O Lᴏʀᴅ, not to us, but to your name bring glory on
account of your steadfast love and your faithfulness.

2 How can the nations say, 'Where then is your God?'

3 when our God is in the heavens, and his work is all that he wills?

4 The idols of the nations are silver and gold, the work of men's
hands.

5 They have mouths but they cannot speak; they have eyes
but they cannot see;

6 they have ears but they cannot hear; they have noses but they
cannot smell;

7 their hands – they cannot touch with them; their feet – they
cannot walk on them; they cannot make a sound in their
throats.

8 Those who make them will become like them, as will all who
trust in them.

9 O Israel! Trust in the Lᴏʀᴅ! He is their helper and their defence.

10 O house of Aaron! Trust in the Lᴏʀᴅ! He is their helper and their
defence.

11 O you that fear the Lᴏʀᴅ! Trust in the Lᴏʀᴅ! He is their helper
and their defence.

12 The Lᴏʀᴅ remembers us, he will bless us; he will bless the house
of Israel, he will bless the house of Aaron;

13 he will bless those who fear the Lᴏʀᴅ, both the small and the
great together.

14 May the Lᴏʀᴅ add to you, to you and to your sons!

<sup>15</sup> May you be blessed by the Lᴏʀᴅ, the worker of the heavens and the earth!

<sup>16</sup> The heavens are the heavens of the Lᴏʀᴅ, but the earth he gave to the sons of man.

<sup>17</sup> The dead do not praise the Lᴏʀᴅ, nor do any who go down into silence.

<sup>18</sup> But we, we will bless the Lᴏʀᴅ, from now until eternity! Hallelujah!

Psalm 114 was about the formation of identity through shared memory; Psalm 115 shapes identity through a series of opposites.

We define who we are sometimes by saying what we are not. I recall one girl starting at our school. Her name was Lucinda. When we asked what she would like us to call her – Lu, Lucy, Cindy, and so on – she insisted she didn't mind. Frustrated, we asked her what she *didn't* want us to call her. 'Sarah!' she announced, much to our surprise. It was only then that we learned she had a twin sister of that name.

Sometimes it's easier to talk about God by talking about what he's *not*, rather than what he *is*. That is to say, we realize we cannot ever actually grasp God because he's so much bigger than we can begin to think about. He's beyond our words, can't be held in our understanding. He fills everything, yet nothing can ever contain him – qualities on which Augustine meditated in his *Confessions*.

Sometimes we define ourselves by what we're not: our politics, our beliefs, our backgrounds. We deny the other sides of an argument to defend our own standpoint. We underline our own sense of self (and self-worth) by asserting, out loud or in our hearts, 'But *I'm* not like that!'

There are two sets of contrasts like this in Psalm 115. There's the contrast between the nations and the Hebrews; and the contrast between God and the idols of the nations.

Let's start with God. Just one verse (verse 3) is given to describing what he *is*: God is 'in the heavens' (that is to say, he's beyond our reach) and 'his work is all that he wills'. That last phrase is hard to translate. It could simply mean 'he does what he wants', a claim typical of any ancient Near Eastern king. But I suspect it goes deeper than that. The Hebrew word here for 'what he *wants*' is emotionally charged – this is more than regal whim. It is what truly gives God delight, what he *wills*. Then because God is so powerful, when he *wills* something, it comes to be. At the creation, all he has to do is say 'Let there be light' and there is light. He *wills* creation into being. Since the Hebrew word for 'doing' also means 'making', this brings the act of creation closer still.

God is one whose will is creative power, whose true delight makes things happen. Not so the idols, who by contrast are given five verses. Describing these idols, the Psalmist is pointing out what God is *not*. Whereas God is one who *makes*, the idols of verses 4–8 are *made*. In verses 3 and 4 the vocabulary overlaps. God creates; the idols are creatures. The uncreated God is capable of all things; the man-made idols can do absolutely nothing. They may be finely sculpted, with detailed features, but what is the point of that if they are entirely impotent? The nations' imagined mocking question to the Hebrews, 'Where is your God?', is turned around. God is completely powerful even as the idols are completely powerless.

The Psalmist gives up on the nations. He has brushed them aside with their pointless questions and useless idols. By talking about the nations and their foolish ways, he highlights what matters to the Hebrews and their religious identity.

As in the earlier Hallel psalms, there's repetition, a sign that this is a memorable and readily performable text designed for worship. Verses 5–7 use an identical structure to describe the idols' features. Verses 9–11 repeat one single command to three different but overlapping groups. Israel – all of God's people; the house of Aaron – the descendants of the first priest of all Israel; and 'you that fear the LORD'. They are all alike directed, 'Trust in the LORD!' This is in exact contradiction to the nations, who would destroy themselves by putting their trust in their man-made idols.

Verses 12–13 unfold this 'trust in the LORD'. These same groups of the faithful are now blessed by God's remembrance of them. Psalm 114 focused on man's remembering God. In Psalm 115 what matters is God remembering man. When God remembers his faithful people, blessings follow.

The common 'doing/making' word appears again. 'The LORD' is the one who has made the heavens and the earth (verse 15); rather than 'maker' here we have 'worker'. This is a God who continues to make, who goes on working in the interests of his creation. The creation is not yet fully finished, it is not yet perfected. Jesus spoke of his 'work'. So can we. We are to be creative alongside the Creator, to work with the master-worker.

As the psalm nears its end, we begin to wonder who is in the limelight here: who are the God-fearers who are to be blessed like this? Those who fear God are those who trust in the Lord, those who bless the Lord, those who praise him. The Hallel theme returns. The speaker commits himself and all his companions to praising God from now until eternity. This is an incredible promise, which only makes sense if we realize that the words of praise are passed down through generations. This people exists through the ages: individuals are limited by death, but the greater community hopes and works for eternity. Their identity lies in their togetherness, their shared responsibility to praise God.

Perhaps at the Last Supper this was an encouraging thought for Jesus. As he faced death, he faced these words claiming that death silenced praise. Yet Jesus' own death was the greatest way to extend praise into all eternity.

We – and our descendants – can praise the Lord. That very possibility, that invitation, is something else we should praise him for.

*Are there things, or people, that you idolize?*

# Maundy Thursday

---

## Psalm 116

¹ I love the Lᴏʀᴅ who hears my voice and my supplications,

² because he has turned his ear to me, so all my days I will call upon him.

³ They surrounded me, the cords of death and the straits of Sheol, a straitjacket caught me and I met with torment.

⁴ So on the name of the Lᴏʀᴅ I cried, 'I beseech you, O Lord, help me escape with my life!'

⁵ Gracious is the Lᴏʀᴅ, and just; our God has compassion.

⁶ Protecting the naive, the Lᴏʀᴅ saved me when I was brought down.

⁷ O my soul, return to quietness, for the Lᴏʀᴅ has settled up for you.

⁸ For you have snatched my soul from death, my eye from tears, and my foot from stumbling.

⁹ I shall walk before the Lᴏʀᴅ in the land of the living.

¹⁰ I was firm in my faith even when I said, 'I am deeply bowed down.'

¹¹ I said in my alarm, 'Every man is a liar.'

¹² How shall I pay the Lᴏʀᴅ back all he has settled up for me?

¹³ I shall take the cup of salvation and upon the name of the Lᴏʀᴅ I shall call.

¹⁴ My vows to the Lᴏʀᴅ I shall make good now in front of all his people.

¹⁵ Valued in the eyes of the Lᴏʀᴅ is the death of those devoted to him.

¹⁶ I beseech you, Lᴏʀᴅ, for I am your servant; I am your servant, the son of your handmaid; you have loosed my bonds.

¹⁷ To you I will offer an offering of thanksgiving, and on the name of the Lᴏʀᴅ will I call.

¹⁸ My vows to the Lᴏʀᴅ I shall make good now in front of all his people,

¹⁹ in the courts of the house of the Lᴏʀᴅ, in the midst of you, O Jerusalem. Hallelujah!

We've been looking ahead to Jesus' Last Supper. Now we're here.

The Gospel accounts of the Last Supper see Jesus through the lens of the Passover sacrifice of the lamb whose blood, poured out, protected God's people in Egypt and enabled them to go free. We can't be sure how far Jesus saw himself in this way. What we can be confident about is that this was a precious ceremony which meant a lot to Jesus and his followers. It was a special and solemn feast, now imbued with richer significance still. Although it may not have been celebrated on the eve of Passover itself – for that in fact was the next day – it's clear that everyone there understood this evening as a Passover supper.

A Passover or Seder meal today involves special foods: for instance bitter herbs symbolizing the bitterness of slavery, and unleavened bread representing the haste of the first Passover meal, broken to re-enact the brokenness of the Israelites' spirits in captivity in Egypt. Four cups of wine memorialize God's four promises of the redemption of his people from slavery in Exodus 6.6–7. It's an evening celebration that moves from brokenness and bitterness to healing. Talk of a return to quietness is like the restored peace of the childlike soul in Psalm 131, and the beautiful, simple wholeness that represents.

Jesus is in charge of this particular Passover meal, making it the first Holy Communion or Eucharist. 'Do this in remembrance of me,' he says, breaking the bread (which he calls 'my body') and taking the cup of wine (which he calls 'my blood of the new covenant'). Jesus now plugs himself into that salvation story we've seen unfolding through the Hallel psalms.

Jesus becomes part of that very salvation story. He takes his place even within the psalms he's singing. We've seen memory aids –

repetitions and rhythms – in the Hallel psalms. But Jesus is not just singing them by heart; he is singing them *in* his heart tonight. He would have sung this psalm many times. What might it have meant for him in the context of the Passover, and this Passover in particular? What might it mean for us in our Maundy Thursday remembrances?

This is a solemn ceremony. The cup of salvation (verse 13) and the thanksgiving offering (verse 17) fit with the idea that the Lord's Supper is a perpetual Holy Thanksgiving, or Eucharist. Knowing it is his last supper, Jesus takes 'the cup of salvation' – not a beautiful silver chalice, but probably a simple pottery cup, standing for rescue from suffering, from death (verses 8–9). This is the new covenant pledged between God and his people, and to endure for all time. See how many times that covenant name of God, 'the LORD', is used here. This new relationship is vowed by God in Jesus, who would have sung verses 14 and 18 with particular poignancy. It doesn't depend upon fragile humanity to keep up impossibly high standards of good behaviour. Jesus lifts the cup, he pours out his blood tonight – as he will tomorrow his life – and he makes vows. This cup calls us to remember Jesus, his vows, and God's pledged relationship with us.

We too make vows and pledge relationships. The baptismal vows made for us at our christening, which we make for ourselves at our confirmation. Our vows to future partners at weddings or civil part-nerships. Our ministerial vows (usually remembered each year on Maundy Thursday in the local cathedral). The promises children make when they join the Guides or Scouts. The contract we sign when we start a job. Politicians are often accused of 'going back on their promises', but we're all in danger of doing it. We could prayer-fully remake all our vows daily with the response 'With the help of God, I will'. The Psalmist keeps his vow to worship, and he's doing it with God, there in the holiest, most special place he can find – the Temple in Jerusalem.

The Temple was *almost* the end of Jesus' journey that night. The Mount of Olives is a stone's throw from the Temple; Jesus was taken all over the place after his arrest, to be questioned, tried and finally condemned, dying just outside the walls of Jerusalem. It seems that the closest Jesus came to the Temple was the house – or prison – of the high priest. Jesus – who had just acted as priest – ended up *not* being in the Temple. In the last hours of Jesus' life, during his arrest and various trials, the Temple was an unforgettable presence – and an unforgettable absence.

Wasn't it odd, then, that Jesus prayed about singing vows to the Lord in the Temple? It's deeper than that. In John's Gospel, just before the Passover, Jesus talks about his body as a temple (John 2). That would have been enough to upset any of the religious authorities. But if Jesus sang Psalm 116 after his Passover meal, mindful of his vows, his commitment to God to save his people by giving his whole life even to death, then the only place he could think of doing that was precisely there – *in the Temple that his incarnate, bodily life actually was.*

These are Jesus' vows. That's literally Jesus' *devotedness* (verse 15). Jesus fulfils his vows freely, willingly. Look at the start of Psalm 116. It's the language of narrowness, bonds, tight corners, straits of distress. This act of rescue demands more than the Psalmist can pay back, more than any of us can pay back. Only the fulfilment of Jesus' vows can settle these accounts. From being in bonds in the opening lines of Psalm 116, God brings freedom. We are freed to offer true thanksgiving.

Vows are binding, but liberating too. God's vows mean even more than our most heartfelt promises. Tonight Jesus makes his vows to God, and God makes his vows to us. And he keeps them.

*What vows do you keep?*

# Good Friday

———•◆•———

## Psalm 117

1 Praise the Lᴏʀᴅ, all you nations! Commend him, all you peoples!
2 For towering over us is his love, and his faithfulness endures for ever. Hallelujah!

## Psalm 118

1 Give thanks to the Lᴏʀᴅ because he is good; for eternal is his steadfast love.
2 Let Israel say, 'Eternal is his steadfast love!'
3 Let the house of Aaron say, 'Eternal is his steadfast love!'
4 Let those who fear the Lᴏʀᴅ say, 'Eternal is his steadfast love!'
5 From the straits I called on the Lᴏʀᴅ; the Lᴏʀᴅ answered me by bringing me out into a spacious place.
6 The Lᴏʀᴅ is with me; I am not afraid; what can any human being do to me?
7 The Lᴏʀᴅ is with me as my helper; as for me I shall look my enemies in the eyes.
8 It is better to take refuge in the Lᴏʀᴅ than to trust in any human being.
9 It is better to take refuge in the Lᴏʀᴅ than to trust in the nobility.
10 All nations have surrounded me; by the name of the Lᴏʀᴅ I shall cut them off.
11 They have surrounded me, truly surrounded me; by the name of the Lᴏʀᴅ I shall cut them off.

12    They have surrounded me like bees! But they are practically
      already extinguished like a burning thorn bush; by the name of
      the Lᴏʀᴅ I shall cut them off.

13    I was pushed, pushed to the point of falling; but the Lᴏʀᴅ
      helped me.

14    The Lᴏʀᴅ is my strength and my song; he has become my
      salvation.

15    Joyful cries of salvation resound in the tents of the righteous:
      'The right hand of the Lᴏʀᴅ has exercised power!

16    The right hand of the Lᴏʀᴅ is raised high; the right hand of the
      Lᴏʀᴅ has exercised power!'

17    I shall not die, for I will live and tell out the works of the Lᴏʀᴅ.

18    The Lᴏʀᴅ disciplined me, truly disciplined me; but he did not
      hand me over to death.

19    Open up for me the gates of righteousness: so may I enter
      them and thank the Lᴏʀᴅ.

20    This is the gateway to the Lᴏʀᴅ: the righteous enter through it.

21    So may I thank you, for you have answered me and have
      become my salvation.

22    The stone the builders threw aside has become the most
      important cornerstone.

23    This is the Lᴏʀᴅ's doing; it is a wonder in our view!

24    This is the day that the Lᴏʀᴅ has made – let us be joyful and
      glad in it!

25    Please, Lᴏʀᴅ, save us, we pray! Please, Lᴏʀᴅ, make us successful,
      please!

26    Blessed is the man who enters in the name of the Lᴏʀᴅ. We
      bless you from the house of the Lᴏʀᴅ.

27    The Lᴏʀᴅ is God! He has given us light! Bind the festal offering
      to the horns of the altar with twine.

28    You are my God and I will give you thanks; you are my God, let
      me exalt you.

29    Give thanks to the Lᴏʀᴅ because he is good; for eternal is his
      steadfast love.


The vows of Psalm 116 are fulfilled as the Hallel sequence unfolds. The praise promised in the Temple is publicly enacted in

Psalms 117 and 118. In Psalm 118 the repeated 'eternal is his stead-fast love' is a shortened form of Psalm 117, imagined in many different voices. The Temple was the avowed setting of Psalm 116; Psalms 117 and 118 conjure up this scene with immediacy.

Psalm 117.2 describes God's mighty love for us. 'Towering over us' brings out the sense of something bold and strong, of protection above us. It evokes the greatness of the Temple building as the Psalmist looks up to its massive walls from just outside. This imagined setting also makes sense of the address to the 'nations' which is seen in Psalm 118, as the Psalmist finally makes good his entry to the Temple, edging ever closer to the heart of the sacred.

Psalm 118, the culmination of the Great Hallel, weaves together ideas from recent psalms. The sequence Israel/house of Aaron/those who fear the Lord (118.2–4) echoes Psalm 115.9–13. The idea of the straits of distress (118.5) resonates with Psalm 116.3.

Picking up on such themes completes Psalms 113–118 as a collection. Repetitions interlace the whole sequence with memorable phrases and similar thoughts. Drawing our attention to how phrases from the Psalms were used and reused, this makes us think about how the Psalms, common words of prayer and worship, could be remembered and repeated. The old becomes new each time. Building up layers of repetition and remembrance makes prayers richer, adds layers of significance and meaning.

It's appropriate that Jesus instituted the Lord's Supper amid repeated Jewish songs and prayers. What would become Holy Communion for Christians was already based on acts and prayers repeated and remembered, made new each time. Every time we eat the bread and drink the wine we are remembering Christ's Passion. We enter Holy Week whenever we celebrate the sacrament of the Eucharist, opening ourselves anew to the Easter story.

The Psalms are songs and prayers of remembrance with future hope. So the Eucharist is an act of remembrance helping us look forward to resurrection life. A lot of Psalm 118 calls to mind not only earlier Hallel psalms, but also other parts of the Jewish tradition. The call to trust (verses 8–9) doesn't just continue ideas in Psalm 115; it connects back to the Old Testament prophets' call to God's people to trust in God, and the accounts in the Old Testament histories of what happens when Israel either trusts or doesn't trust in God. The burning thorn bush (verse 12) makes us think of the burning bush at the call of Moses (Exodus 3). On Good Friday, it also reminds us of Christ's crown of thorns.

Psalm 118 is also remembered and repeated in Christian traditions, especially at Easter. Verse 22 is put word for word – in the usual Greek translation – into the mouth of Jesus in the Synoptic Gospels (Matthew 21.42; Mark 12.10; Luke 20.17) after his entry into Jerusalem, when he is telling the parable of the tenants in the vineyard. Arrested shortly afterwards, Jesus is pictured as that rejected cornerstone. Verse 26 gives us the full 'Benedictus' of our Holy Communion service. Verse 24 has been used throughout the ages to meditate on the day of resurrection in sermons and music. Verse 14 is word for word the first verse of an Easter canticle, Moses' song after the crossing of the Red Sea at the exodus after the first Passover (Exodus 15).

The repeated word 'salvation' in these texts makes us remember that this is effectively the name of Jesus. Yeshua, Joshua, Jesus, salvation – all are from the same root in Hebrew. When Christians talk of 'Jesus our Saviour' we're repeating ourselves. It helps make the point that Jesus is our salvation, and in Psalm 118 God 'has become my salvation' (verses 14, 21).

In verse 15, salvation is related to God's right hand. God's right hand stands for his strength. For us, to be someone's right hand, or at someone's right hand, is to be the henchman, the primary player in the team. As Christians therefore it's possible to find further meaning here. Jesus is understood to be *at* the right hand of God; so Jesus, salvation, *is* God's right hand. Jesus is the one who achieves salvation, the one who enacts God's mighty victories. 'Joyful sounds of salvation' are truly heard because the 'right hand of God' is active and mighty.

The festal offering of verse 27 fits with this. Jewish rituals in the Old Testament period involved various kinds of sacrifice, often performed to set right the relationship between God and humanity after sin had been committed. Reading this psalm at the Passover feast would have connected the offering specifically with the Passover lamb slaughtered to protect and liberate the Hebrews from their slavery in Egypt. Christians can powerfully extend this meaning: Jesus, sacrificed at the Passover, became the Passover lamb to protect and liberate all God's people from various slaveries. The detail of binding the offering recalls the binding of Isaac, Abraham's only son (Genesis 22). Binding the festal offering with twine loudly resonates with the idea of God's only Son, Jesus, as the sacrifice to fix the relationship between God and humanity for all time.

That twine used to bind the sacrifice is rope made from plant material. It's not so far-fetched to imagine it was made from woven palms. Palm branches were cast down before Jesus on Palm Sunday, celebrating his entry into Jerusalem. Similar cords now bind the sacrificial victim. Connections continue in verses 19, 20 and 26, with hints of another Temple entrance liturgy (like Psalm 24).

The Psalmist prays vehemently (verse 25). So can we. The Hebrew word *na* is like saying 'please!' or 'I pray!' The phrase 'save us! please!' is the Hebrew *hosanna*. Palm Sunday's 'hosanna!' is a prayer – God, save us! Jesus, save us! – so we can enter with Jesus into this most holy place.

On Good Friday we enter fully into Jesus' Passion.

*Choose a word or phrase from today's psalms and repeat it quietly and slowly to yourself for between 5 and 15 minutes. You might want to say it out loud, or whisper it, or mouth it, or just think it again and again. You might find that setting a timer helps you feel freer to concentrate. If your mind wanders, be kind to yourself, don't worry about it, and just bring yourself back to your word or phrase whenever you notice your attention has slipped. How does this word or phrase change you?*

# Holy Saturday

———•◦•———

## Selah

The mysterious and faith are connected. At the heart of faith is mystery. Like clouds of incense, some things in faith remain cloudy, unclear. There always will be such things. Faith is not dogmatic. It is not summed up in one easy textbook or course. It is dynamic, it changes with the seasons, it weathers and adapts. There's always space for the unknown, for mystery.

One mystery of the Psalms is that word *selah*. You may have wondered at it back in Psalms 24, 32, 50, 55 and 88. It pops up at the end of some verses. No one quite knows what it means.

It's the word I've chosen to sit with on Holy Saturday. Not a word about God: because Holy Saturday marks the day that Jesus is dead. He died yesterday just before evening came. He now lies in the grave. How could Christians meditate on God in a world where there is no Jesus?

What we can contemplate is mystery: a mystery that is unsolved and freely, unpredictably reoccurring. *Selah* appears without obvious rhyme or reason. Its meaning is shrouded. Just as Jesus' body is shrouded in the grave today, just as the Passion narrative has yet to unfold its meaning in the salvation story, so it remains unclear to our age what *selah* means, what its function is.

It literally means 'lift up' or 'exalt', as in praise (we lift up hands or voices in worship). Yet this doesn't explain why it only occurs at the end of verses. It could indicate a kind of response, a refrain. Yet elsewhere in the Psalms refrains are written out without any problem. It might be a musical direction we just don't understand any more, pointing out a repetition, or a musical interlude, or the introduction of a different group of singers – it occurs more often in the psalms which have musical superscriptions. Yet this isn't always the case.

Or it could mean 'Pause', or 'Silence', setting out a time for reflection.

Different churches and communities recite psalms in different ways. Psalms might be sung as songs or hymns, whether a few verses or the whole text. They might be read with a repeated refrain. In cathedrals and choral foundations they're often sung to Anglican chant, where one sequence of notes provides the structure, taking two verses in pairs, swapping sides. Religious communities might sing them to a plainsong chant. They can be read gently with pauses halfway through a verse, the sides of the worshipping community taking the verses in turn. Jewish traditions of singing the Psalms are different again. There are all sorts of ways of singing these Songs of the Spirit.

Whatever *selah* meant to the earliest Jewish communities, it is a gift to us now. Seeing it in the Psalms reminds us that we'll probably never get to the bottom of what any ancient biblical text means. It reminds us that these are texts on to which our own traditions have been grafted. Above all, it reminds us to stop and reflect. Whether with a musical interlude or in silence, it's important to pause.

Holy Saturday is the day when Jesus stopped. He rested in the grave. Like God resting on the Sabbath day, the seventh day of creation, in Genesis 2. The Ten Commandments enshrined the Sabbath, the day off, the day to stop and think and spend time with God. From time to time, we are all called to 'nothingness', to intentional rest, in our living as well as in our dying. Even in his death Jesus was showing us the way.

So on Holy Saturday I invite you to reflect on *selah*. To pause, to take it in. To let the previous words sink into your heart and mind and life. To share in resting, while Jesus sleeps the sleep of death.

It's sometimes hard to stop. Like being on a bus when it brakes suddenly and the passengers lurch forwards, it can feel that our minds, our hearts, our souls lurch within us when we've been very busy and then come to a standstill, on retreat, or when we stop for a significant amount of prayer time.

We all need to stop sometimes, to re-evaluate our lives. To make sure we're still heading in the right direction. It can be confusing and daunting to stop, especially if busy-ness is one of our coping mechanisms. But stop we must. Jesus goes ahead of us even in that, enacting the most fearful of stoppings as his body, the incarnate body of God, paused in the tomb.

*Selah* is like the silences in music. I have been listening to Bach's *St John Passion* as I write these Holy Week reflections. *Selah* is like that silence at the end, when the singers close their scores, the band puts down their instruments and the conductor drops his hands. A moment where we wonder at what has gone before, and that it is now finished.

Holy Week is at an end. *Selah* can be for Christians a moment in retelling Jesus' story where we pause, still ourselves and wonder – at the mystery of what has gone before, is now finished, and is yet unfolding.

*What is the question you most want to ask, and how do you live with not knowing the answer?*

# WEEK 7: EASTER

## A redeemed world

# Easter Day

## Psalm 103

1 Of David. O my soul, bless the Lord! All my inward being,
 praise his holy name!
2 O my soul, bless the Lord, and do not forget all his generous
 doings!
3 He is the one who forgives all your wrongdoings, who heals
 any and all of your diseases.
4 He is the one who redeems your life from the Pit, the one who
 crowns you with steadfast love and compassion.
5 He is the one who fills your life with good, renewing your
 youth like an eagle's.
6 The Lord does righteous deeds and acts of justice for all who
 are oppressed.
7 He made known his ways to Moses, to the people of Israel his
 deeds.
8 Compassionate and full of grace is the Lord, slow to anger, and
 rich in steadfast love.
9 Not for ever will he be the accuser, not for ever will he keep his
 anger.
10 He does not act towards us as our sins deserve, he does not
 pay us back according to our guilt.
11 Because as the heavens tower over the earth, so his steadfast
 love towers over those who fear him.
12 As far as the east is from the west, this far away from us has he
 put our transgressions.

13   As a father is compassionate to his children, this compassionate
    is the Lord to those who fear him.

14   Because he, he knows what we are made of, he remembers
    that we are dust.

15   As for humanity – its days are like grass; like the flower in the
    field it flourishes;

16   because a wind passes it and it becomes as nothing; even its
    own place no longer regards it.

17   But the steadfast love of the Lord is from everlasting to
    everlasting to those who fear him, and his righteousness
    to their children's children,

18   to those who keep his covenant and those who remember to
    do his bidding.

19   The Lord in the heavens has set up his throne, and his kingdom
    rules over all.

20   Bless the Lord, you angels of his, you mighty ones who do his
    word, who listen to the voice of his word!

21   Bless the Lord, all his hosts, you ministers of his who do his will!

22   Bless the Lord, all his works, from every place in his realm!
    O my soul, bless the Lord!

Easter is a time of surprises. Just when the disciples thought it was all over, really all over, there were new adventures, new miracles – many more things to get their heads round. They'd thought that trying to grasp all the mysteries of Jesus' teaching was hard enough. Now they had to grapple with an immense new life experience, new to the whole world: the resurrection.

What is surprising can begin to make sense, if we sit with it long enough. But we have to get past doubt, shock, confusion, fear, dumbfoundedness and so on first. If something has been yearned for, dreamed about, it can be mind-boggling if and when it actually arrives. It's hard to believe that we've actually made it: this is real, not just a far-off hope. In the resurrection accounts it's worth noticing that joy does not come immediately. The surprise of the Easter news would have taken Jesus' family and friends a while to accept. We know what mind-blowing can feel like. This was mind-blowing beyond any expectations.

The resurrection isn't just a medical surprise: it's not a resuscitation, a bringing back to life. Resurrection is a wholly new thing. Not just life after death – that would have been yesterday – but now *life after* life after death. Jesus' body is transformed. The old, broken, buried body is made new. Jesus is both unrecognizable and fully recognizable. This body can appear upstairs and behind closed doors. This body is a new creation, in continuity with the old, but replacing the old. It's a new substance, new existence, wholly new life.

New life – in continuity with old life – is apt at this time of year. Picture sitting on a rocky outcrop on a steeply sloping Dorset field in springtime. Old familiar noises become many new songs – the varieties of birdsong, the hum of the occasional early bee, the barely audible flicker of a butterfly's wings. The dead grasses and the bare branches are still visible beneath the new growth. The climb up to these ancient mossy rocks: Christ's stumbling to his high-up, stony Calvary hill was a path to a place of new life. Sheep and shepherds pastured in the field below have had one male lamb removed from the flock to be the Easter lamb: Christ, the Lamb, was sacrificed as the festal offering.

The old is rejuvenated each spring. The old stories of the Bible are heard afresh in Christ. The old songs of the Temple are fitting for Christian Lent and Easter reflection as well as for the most solemn Jewish worship. Easter liturgies seen before are performed anew. Old and new go hand in hand both in the Psalms and at Easter: together they can surprise us.

Sunday, the first day of the week: in Jerusalem it's back to work time, as it is for the newly risen Jesus. The work of Psalm 103 is blessing: a task given not to us alone but to the whole creation. It's hard to convey the Hebrew word order in smooth English, but the phrases where the Psalmist addresses himself repeatedly (verses 1–2, 22) are 'Bless, O my soul, the LORD'. The blessing, 'the LORD', and the self are muddled together in overflowing rejoicing. It is surprising that all God's 'works' are involved in the work of blessing; we realize we are blessed daily by the natural world as well as by one another.

There is cause for exultant, jubilant, overwhelming praise: the words the Psalmist uses have weight and unstoppable joy. The Psalmist describes a salvation story and applies it to us (verses 3–5). God has forgiven our wrongs, healed our wounds. He 'redeems life . . . from the Pit': the pit of the prison, the pit of the grave. Thanks to God's 'generous doings' (verse 2), this is our redemption story. An Easter reading is that this generosity is God's pouring out of himself in Jesus, his ministry, his Passion, crucifixion and resurrection. Thanks to all this, we are forgiven, healed, redeemed – from our captivity, from our lowest points, from our deaths, giving us new life.

Remember: a 'redeemer' is a family member (Psalm 107). So in Psalm 103 the Redeemer is the God who makes himself one of our family – making God the most compassionate father possible. The Lord's perfect justice is surprising in its utter generosity, both in Psalm 103 and in Christ. New and old sit alongside one another: the teaching of ancient Moses (verse 7) alongside the renewed, youthful life of an eagle (verse 5). This justice follows on from the old, yet seems to turn back the clock. In the new life of Easter, the old notion of God as Redeemer becomes even more significant. It's not just that we're welcomed into the family of God (Psalm 23). God has become a member of our family. Avoid taking that for granted: let it be surprising. This is true compassion for our need for salvation from our sins (verses 8–12).

Verses 13–18 are often heard at funeral services. In the midst of life we are in death; in the midst of death we are in life. We have still to die; but through our dying we have the hope of full life in Christ. The kingdom of God is already here, in the resurrection of Christ; and yet it is also not yet here, because there is still death, suffering, injustice in our world. As Easter week unfolds we will see the mingling of these truths, and discover how that helps us to look forward to the new, however surprising it might be.

We get used to the old order of things. Let's make sure Easter doesn't become an 'old truth' for us: let it be ever new, as we and the whole of God's creation are continually renewed. Recognizing and rejoicing in surprises is one way of hearing the voice of God, seeing God at work, knowing him to be active in our lives. Being open to surprise helps us hear good news and begin to believe what is unbelievably good.

*Think of something special you've begun to take for granted. Can you wonder at it again?*

# Easter Monday

───◆───

## Psalm 145

1. A song of praise. Of David. Let me worship you, my God the King! And let me bless your name for ever and ever!

2. Every day, let me bless you, and let me praise your name for ever and ever!

3. Great is the Lord, and utterly praiseworthy! He is so great no one can get their head around it!

4. Generation to generation will praise your actions; and they shall declare how mighty you are.

5. The splendid glory of your majesty, and your wonderful acts – let me meditate on these.

6. The people shall speak of the power of your fearsome acts; let me retell how great you are!

7. They shall pour out words which remember your immense goodness, and they shall shout with joy about the way you enact justice.

8. Gracious and compassionate is the Lord; he is slow to get angry and has huge loving-kindness.

9. The Lord is good to all, and his compassion extends over his whole creation.

10. All your creatures will praise you, O Lord, and your faithful ones will bless you.

11. The glory of your kingdom, they shall speak of that; and your power, they shall put that into words too.

12. To declare God's importance to the sons of man, and the glorious splendour of his kingdom.

<sup>13</sup> Your kingdom is a kingdom that shall last for ever, and your rule is for all generations.

<sup>14</sup> The LORD supports all those who fall, and lifts up all those who are bowed down.

<sup>15</sup> The eyes of all are upon you, they are hoping in you, and you are the one who regularly gives them their food,

<sup>16</sup> opening out your hand, and fulfilling the hungers of every living thing.

<sup>17</sup> The LORD is right in all his ways, and kind in all his deeds.

<sup>18</sup> Near is the LORD to all who call on him, to all who call on him in truth.

<sup>19</sup> He settles the hunger of all who fear him, he hears those who cry out to be saved and he saves them.

<sup>20</sup> The LORD keeps watch over all who love him, and he will completely destroy the wicked enemies.

<sup>21</sup> My mouth shall utter the praise of the LORD, and all flesh shall bless his holy name for ever and ever.

The truth begins to sink in.

Have you ever noticed how, when something dawns on us slowly, it starts to make sense of a whole lot of things we couldn't figure out before? Like saying to a friend or loved one, 'Ah, thank you for telling me that. Now I understand why you did this, and how that happened . . . It didn't make sense until now.'

It's like that when Jesus appears to two disciples on the road to Emmaus (Luke 24). The disciples don't yet recognize Jesus, but their travelling companion, whoever he is, helps them make sense of what's been going on in Jerusalem these last few days. Exploring the Scriptures along the journey, finally breaking bread together, they slowly grasp more and more truth of Jesus' story and consequently of their own. That gradual comprehension no doubt continued through their lives, through the retelling of these stories, in conversation and the written word.

Look at verse 7. It sums up the whole of Psalm 145 – and many other psalms, for that matter. The people will remember God's immense goodness. Psalm 145 is a shared meditation on God's goodness, greatness, strength, justice. It is an act of remembrance of all God is and has done so far.

But it isn't specific. Unlike some psalms that tell particular stories (Psalm 114 and the exodus, for example), Psalm 145 doesn't describe individual instances of God's goodness or loving-kindness. So we can freely make it our own for contemplation, while sharing it with others – through the generations (verse 4) and the whole creation (verse 9).

This strengthens collective worship. Realizing we each have our own faith stories to bring together, when we praise God as individuals and at the same time as one voice, we encourage one another. We remind one another that God's love for us is not just for me, or you, but for all of us. He has a special relationship with each one of us. He has no favourites. I'm not more holy than you in God's eyes, you're not more righteous than me. By God's grace, by his loving-kindness, we're all able to rejoice in this together – equally.

The idea that our own particular efforts don't pay off for us personally may make us feel aggrieved. That's not fair, is it? But the moment we talk about fairness is the moment that we endanger our community. It's not about deserving, counting up to make things balance. That's not the way God does justice. This is something we begin to learn when we look at Jesus, and the cross.

The idea that we're not always right can wind us up too. To rework an old saying, while I married Mr Right, he would be the first to say that his first name isn't 'Always'. By contrast, God *is* always right. That's what verse 17 claims. Accepting that someone other than us is right can be hard to swallow. Yet it is liberating, as truth is (verse 18). That's a good reason to trust in the truth and to seek it, to surrender ourselves to the true God who is always right.

The idea that God is always, fully, completely right in everything, always, everywhere, is brought out in Psalm 145 by the structure. Like Psalms 25 and 119, this psalm is an acrostic, working through the alphabet verse by verse. You may notice there are only 21 verses, not 22 – one letter is missing (the *nun* verse, which should have been between verses 13 and 14). It's as if the Psalmist is saying, 'All that God is and does is complete, entire and perfect; but I cannot do justice to this. I am a mortal, limited, and no one in this life can ever truly get to the bottom of that.' In verse 3 comes the idea that God is so unutterably great that, well, no one can utter it fully.

The Psalmist does his best, though. This is a God who satisfies our every need. God gives us our food in due season (verse 15), as Christians pray daily in the Lord's Prayer. God fills us up when we hunger (verse 16). Perhaps that's a hunger for peace, or justice: it's not only a hunger for food. Hungering for the good things of the world (for peace in conflict-ridden countries, or justice for the poor in our own cities), we are not immediately satisfied, but it's a first step to participating in God's justice in the world.

Praying, hungering for God's justice won't attract everyone. Some of us may be quite comfortable with our cars, houses, lifestyles, dinners out, the jobs we've aimed at for years, the things we really feel we've earned through our own hard work. Why should others who haven't worked as hard as we have get the same? God's justice sees the whole context better than we ever could. Remember, he's always right. He knows the things that have held some back – poverty, ill health, lack of support when they needed it most, and so on. He takes that into account. This is a new balance sheet of whether something's 'fair' or not. Only God can judge what is truly fair.

That, then, is the kingdom of God for which we pray; the kingdom which we need to pray we can get our heads around. This is the kingdom (verses 11–13) into which we are all invited; this is the kingdom for which in truth we should all yearn.

Let me worship you like this, my God and my King! There are two ways of translating these phrases: 'Let me' or 'I will'. If you're at a stage in faith where you're not sure you can confidently pray for God's kingdom, but that you certainly *want* to want it, then praying 'Let me praise the glorious splendour of your kingdom!' is a very good starting point (verses 1, 2, 5 and 6). The more we do so, the more sense it will all make, and the better (verse 21) we can pray 'I will.'

*'Hindsight is a wonderful thing.' Can you think of something which didn't make sense at the time, but which you later realized was God being right?*

# Easter Tuesday

---

## Psalm 146

1   Hallelujah! O my soul, praise the God Who Is!
2   May I praise the LORD as long as I live; oh that I might make music to God throughout my whole life!
3   May you not put your trust in nobles, in the son of Adam, in whom there is no salvation.
4   His breath departs, he returns to his adamant; on that day his thoughts perish.
5   Blessed is he who has the God of Jacob for his helper, whose hope is on the LORD his God.
6   He made sky and earth, the sea and all that is in them, the one who keeps faithfulness for ever;
7   the one who makes judgement for those who are oppressed; the one who gives food to the hungry; the LORD who sets free those who have been bound;
8   the LORD who opens up the blind; the LORD who raises up those who have been bent down; the LORD who loves those who are just.
9   The LORD who watches over refugees, he restores orphan and widow, he bends back on itself the way of the wicked.
10   The LORD will reign for ever: your God, O Zion, to generation and generation! Hallelujah!

'Alleluia, Christ is risen!' 'He is risen indeed, Alleluia!' How do you say this? Do you cry it aloud confidently, 'Hallelu-jah!', encouraging others in the congregation to praise the Lord, retelling again and again the good news of the resurrection? Or do you say it just like any old congregational response in church – one that perhaps doesn't seem to require much thought? And if there is a deeper meaning to this well-known liturgical saying, what other deeper meanings might be available to us in our worship that we haven't necessarily thought hard about before?

These last five psalms in the Psalter all begin with the 'Hallelujah' call to praise. It's even more persistent than in the Hallel series, Psalms 113–118. But it's not only about exhorting one another to praise God. It's also self-encouragement. The Psalmist addresses his own soul (verse 1). He is a member of the great congregation. As we did yesterday, we can see the mutuality of the Church here – it is one and many, self and others, at the same time.

We tend to joke that talking to ourselves is a sign of madness. But it could be like the moment, on finding something we'd lost, when we breathe out, 'Thank God!' We express relief and gratitude for our good luck, but we also remember to be thankful.

We need perpetual reminders to be thankful: we can use that moment when we've caught the bus in the nick of time, or arrived at our favourite place, or heard a good story, to stop for a moment and express our gratitude.

The Psalmist exhorts himself and others simultaneously. The speaker is reflecting, trying to keep himself on track; he's also the teacher, reminding others about God who is Creator and helper.

Remembering creation themes, the 'son of man', or 'son of Adam', *ben Adam*, comes up again, as in Psalms 8 and 90. The Psalmist is himself a son of Adam; and he knows as a man himself that no person – not even ourselves – should be trusted as we trust God. Think back to Psalms 115 and 118. The only person who can hold such trust is the Lord God of Jacob.

Man, the son of Adam, is contrasted with God. Man is earthly, God is heavenly. Someone born of the adamant, of the unyielding earth, cannot have all the answers, provide every help. Salvation belongs to God. Salvation can't come from the creature, only from the Creator.

Yet the 'God of Jacob' is a God associated with human beings. And a literally crooked one at that: 'Jacob' in Hebrew is all about crooked-ness, connecting with the stories about his birth (grasping the heel, the crooked part of the body of his elder twin Esau, in Genesis 25) and about how he stole Esau's birthright (Genesis 27). Jacob's role in the salvation story is pivotal: wrestling with God himself (Genesis 32), Jacob receives the new name 'Israel', a name to be given to a whole people.

God is not just one who creates. He is referred to in Psalm 146 in terms of his actions. A string of participles lists his abilities – not just what he can do, but what he *cares* to do, *chooses* to do for his people. Creation and every act of redemption are related; they sit on a continuum. Every saving moment is like a re-creation, new direction and new life.

It's that 'doing/making' verb again. God is the God who does creation, who makes creation (verse 6). He does, and makes, justice (verse 7). Justice is an act of creation. God's a giver, of food to the hungry. He's a liberator, setting free those who are bound. He's a healer (verse 8): an opener of blind eyes, a raiser-up of those who are bent over. He's a carer for those who are needy (verse 9): he's a protector of travellers or strangers, he helps up orphans and the widow.

Scattered among these descriptions of God in his just acts, he's a lover of the righteous (verse 8), one who derails the wicked (verse 9). There's much language about crookedness in these verses, of making the bent straight: it makes sense that here God is not only the Creator God, but the God of Jacob.

God creates and he sets things straight. In verse 10, the Psalmist extols God's rule. This is the straightness of the best king, the only ruler who can be trusted. Even the poetry bends back on itself. Set this straight ruler against the untrustworthy princes of verse 4: you see such a straight ruler that his realm extends to the horizon and beyond, through the generations. There is no crookedness about God, or about his ways.

This is the God of the plumb line of Amos (Amos 7), the builder God who has a spirit-level, who sets up cities straight. In the closing words of Psalm 146, the Psalmist addresses Zion: Jerusalem, the City of God, the people of God. God, the builder, keeps things straight from generation to generation.

It's not always easy to set things straight. Broken bones that have set crooked have to be broken again in order to be set straight. A 'crook' who is set straight will have to leave behind his community and way of life. We might struggle to accept being straightened. In Psalm 146 we are challenged to desire it wholeheartedly.

The redeemed world we celebrate at Easter is a world where God's straight rule reigns supreme. God straightens us, his creation, again and again; in that is redemption. Associating himself even with humanity, the God of Jacob is in Jesus himself bound, echoing verse 7. Jesus, who comes to straighten up the creation once and for all, has his body broken, made crooked, on the cross. That broken body, set upright in the resurrection, is the image of creation redeemed.

*What makes you say 'Thank God' or 'Alleluia'?*

# Easter Wednesday

---

## Psalm 147

1 Praise the LORD! Because it is good to make music to our God, because it is fun and fitting to sing praise!

2 The LORD builds up Jerusalem and gathers together the exiles of Israel.

3 He is the one who heals those who have broken hearts, he binds up their injuries.

4 He reckons the number of the stars, and he gives names to all of them.

5 Great is our Lord, and immense is his power! As for his wisdom, it cannot be reckoned.

6 The LORD sets those who have been afflicted back on their feet, he brings the wicked down to the ground.

7 Sing to the LORD in a song of thanksgiving! Make music to our God on the lyre!

8 He is the one who covers the heavens with clouds, who provides rain for the earth, who makes mountains grow grass,

9 who gives to cattle their food, and to the young of the raven what they cry for.

10 He is not impressed by the strength of a horse, he does not favour the muscular man;

11 the LORD favours those who fear him, those who wait for his loving-kindness.

12 O Jerusalem, glorify the LORD! Praise your God, O Zion!

13 because he made strong the bars of your gates, he blessed your sons within your walls.

14  He makes your borders well, he satisfies you with the best
    wheat.
15  He is the one who sends his spoken word to the earth; his
    word runs swiftly.
16  He is the one who settles snow like wool, he scatters hoarfrost
    like ashes,
17  he throws his hailstones like crumbs. Who can stand his icy
    cold?
18  Then he sends his word and he melts them; he breathes out
    and the waters flow.
19  He has declared his word to Jacob, his statutes and judgements
    to Israel.
20  He has not acted like this towards any other nation; of such
    judgements they know nothing. Praise the Lord!

This exuberant psalm, like Psalm 146, begins and ends with the
Hallelujah call to praise. The Psalmist is addressing all in his sight;
it's Jerusalem he's particularly thinking about right now (verses 2 and
12). This is undeniably community worship, in which the Psalmist
numbers himself as a participant.

Verse 2 imagines a post-exilic vision: a Jerusalem that needs
rebuilding, whose inhabitants have been exiled and are now returning.
Like the movement between Holy Week and Easter, there's a dreadful
past at the back of the Psalmist's mind, but a wonderful hopeful future
being realized here and now. That is something to rejoice over.

Sometimes it's easier to pray 'thank you' than 'help!' Take me out
of the busy-ness of everyday stresses, into beautiful countryside, into
close companionship with God, and then I do simply want to say
'Thanks be to God!' It's a response to wonder, to awe: those occasions
when we open our eyes, notice glimpses of God all around us, and
manage not to take things for granted. Or it's a reaction to God when
he acts in our lives.

Even some who have no faith say they sometimes want to utter
thanks. The desire to praise is deep in our humanity. Being a Christian is a blessing, because there's always someone to thank with all
our heart and mind and soul – and God, our 'maker and doer', is
someone whom it makes great sense to thank.

Thanks and praise are responses to good things. We notice something good, judge it praiseworthy; we attend to it. We want to attribute its worth to someone. Worship is 'worth-ship': a judgement and response to something good which makes us give thanks and praise.

The restoration of Jerusalem – in which descendants of its former residents were brought back together – was certainly a reason to praise and thank God. This is the God who at one moment is personally tending to those who are hurting (verse 3), and the next is setting the stars in order (verse 4). This is the only true 'maker/doer' or 'Creator/Redeemer'.

The injured to whom the Psalmist refers are probably not those wounded at the sack of Jerusalem, because that took place 50 years before the psalm was composed. Few would have remembered Jerusalem before it was sacked and still been fit enough to be able to return under the Persian king Cyrus in 531 BC. The Old Testament books of Ezra and Nehemiah recount some of the Israelite officials' struggles as they returned to rebuild Jerusalem. It wasn't easy. There was unease between the Hebrews who had stayed in Jerusalem (the Babylonians left behind the poor, the lowest classes) and those who had been deported (the officials, the upper classes, those who held power).

There's good reason to consolidate this sense of belonging together in communal worship. The Psalter as we have it today perhaps indicates as much. Maybe the Psalms were edited at this period, and this closing collection of Hallel psalms was added to the end of the Psalter to fix it all in place. Common praise is a good way to build community. People, text and texts mesh together here, like the alliterative Hebrew pairing translated 'fun and fitting' (verse 1).

In this atmosphere of rebuilding, God is glorified for the strengthening of the city gates (verse 13) and the mending of walls (verse 14). Thanks to God, these walls have *shalom* – one word makes them both well and peaceful. The only enemies mentioned are those regarded alongside the 'afflicted' (verse 6), perhaps a glimpse of angst between factions in the new Jerusalem. By giving thanks to God rather than to any individual leader or group, the Psalmist brings unity in and through worship.

In worship we sing with one voice. We are sharing our songs, sharing our spirit. Psalm 147 is one 'song of thanksgiving' (verse 7), to be sung all together. Different people contribute in different ways – by playing the lyre, for example – but all build up worship and praise as one body.

The days after Easter were crucial for rebuilding the disciples. They would have been battered and afraid, unbelieving and untrusting of one another (think about Thomas, for instance). One minute they were bereaved, the next they were gobsmacked.

Like St Francis, whose life was shaped by God's call to him to 'rebuild my Church', let's think at Easter about how we rebuild our church, our communities, year after year. We've gone through the Passion together, now let's rejoice together. Let's regroup, just like the disciples did. We have different styles of worship, different readings of the Bible, different views about how to run the church – but, inspired by the Psalmist, we can overcome any enmity or divisions. Let's make sure that we are united at this new next stage of our own discipleship.

Luke's account of what happened after the resurrection is given twice: at the end of his Gospel and at the beginning of his sequel, Acts. Jesus tells the disciples to stay in Jerusalem to wait for the Father's promise; when that promise is fulfilled at Pentecost, they receive the Holy Spirit all together. This is a united church.

Waiting for God in our spiritual new Jerusalem of life after Easter, let's sing Psalm 147 with the Psalmist. Praise focusing on the immense power of the Creator/Redeemer goes far beyond individual views. It's a response to the divine view: God's power is depicted as being higher than the clouds, above all weathers (verses 8, 16–18). God who sustains his creation (verses 9, 13, 14) is God who above all provides justice (verses 19–20). This is a defining feature of the identity of God's people.

Are there threats to unity in our churches? Who are we to judge our fellow believers' differing views? God's word gives justice powerfully (verses 15 and 19). That word of God makes Christians think of the beginning of John's Gospel, where Jesus is the Word of God. Let's entrust our unity to him.

*How can you help to rebuild the Church?*

# Easter Thursday

—◆—

## Psalm 148

1  Hallelujah! Praise the LORD from the heavens! Praise him in the heights!
2  Praise him, all his angels! Praise him, all his hosts!
3  Praise him, sun and moon! Praise him, all stars of light!
4  Praise him, highest heavens, and waters which are above the heavens!
5  Let them praise the name of the LORD, because he commanded and they were created.
6  He set them up to last for ever and ever; he gave a decree that will not pass away.
7  Praise the LORD from the earth – you great sea creatures and all the ocean depths,
8  fire and hail, snow and fog, storm wind which carries out his word,
9  mountains and all hills, fruit trees and all cedars,
10 wild animals and all cattle, creeping things and flying birds,
11 kings of the earth and all peoples, princes and all rulers of the earth,
12 young men and young women, old men and young boys –
13 let them praise the name of the LORD because his name alone is sublime, and his majesty over earth and heaven.
14 He has raised up a horn for his people, a song of praise for his faithful ones, for the children of Israel, a people who are near him. Hallelujah!

Most high omnipotent good Lord
To you be ceaseless praise outpoured
And blessing without measure.
From you alone all creatures came
No one is worthy you to name.

My Lord be praised by Brother Sun
Who through the skies his course does run
And shines in brilliant splendour.
With brightness he does fill the day
And signifies your boundless sway.

My Lord be praised by Sister Moon
And all the stars that with her soon
Will point the glitt'ring heavens.
Let wind and air and cloud and calm
And weathers all, repeat the psalm.

By Sister Water then be blessed
Most humble, useful, precious chaste.
Be praised by Brother Fire:
Cheerful is he, robust and bright
And strong to lighten all the night.

By Mother Earth my Lord be praised
Governed by you, she has upraised
What for our life is needful.
Sustained by you through ev'ry hour
She brings forth fruit, and herb, and flower.

St Francis loved singing. As a young troubadour, he sang songs for noble women. After his conversion, he became a troubadour for God, singing songs for his true beloved. These verses are from his most famous song (which we might know better as 'All creatures of our God and King').

This 'Canticle of the Creatures', as it is called, looks like a meditation on Psalm 148. Calling all creation to worship God invites the whole of creation into the worshipping community. Yesterday we thought about how worship brings people together. Better still, today we see how it *unites all creation*. We call every aspect of creation our brother or sister – which helps us see ourselves as creatures. It's part of that levelling humility that remembers that we too are made of the humus, the soil to which we shall one day return.

In Psalm 146 the Psalmist spoke to himself; in Psalm 147 he spoke to the Jerusalem community; now in Psalm 148 he speaks to the cosmic reaches of the universe. From the heavens (verses 1–6) to the earth (verses 7–13), the call to praise is strong and far-reaching. It's not that the Psalmist is pridefully thinking he can address these universal forces; it's that the call to praise can never be contained. True praise resounds throughout the whole created order. That's the vision here.

The humility that levels each of us with all of God's creatures is what fully enables us to see God set apart. Verses 11–12 are like a manifesto of equality. Princes, rulers and plebs, men and women, young and old, all are held together. Grouping everyone together dissolves the social hierarchy, so all can realize that God alone is higher, 'sublime' (verse 13). All alike benefited from God's graciousness when he 'raised up a horn for his people' (verse 14; a way of describing a plenitude of good things, success). Perhaps the equality expressed in the closing verses of Psalm 148 influenced St Paul's words: 'Amongst you there is no longer Jew or Greek, slave or free, male or female: for you are all one in Christ Jesus' (Galatians 3.28).

This is redemption: as God's creatures, we all belong to Christ Jesus. Theologies of the cross include the idea of Jesus paying the price of our sins, settling our debts to God, receiving once and for all the punishment we should have faced, because only Jesus was holy enough to do so. This risks over-emphasizing the idea that God is wrathful and vengeful, which not all Christians find attractive, yet it does articulate the payback idea of redemption. After all, 'redemption' is literally a 'buying back'. A redeemer 'buys back' the redeemed (we talk about redeeming vouchers in shops, for example); this is the act of a kinsman (Psalm 107).

Maybe that shifts our theology of the cross a little. Jesus came on to the level of God's creatures. He became humanity's closest family member, in order to redeem, buy back, humankind. He re-purchased humankind for God. So we belong to God. God has invested in us. We really are 'in' Christ Jesus; we've been made members of God's family. Or, in the words of the closing verse of today's psalm, we are truly God's people, God's 'faithful ones', 'a people who are near him'. You don't get closer than flesh and blood.

Another way of understanding what it means that Christ died for us is that he took part in our lives so we could take part in his: a kind of interchange – more interwoven than a simple exchange. Jesus came alongside humanity, he integrated with humankind, took humanity on himself and died. He alone, fully God as well as fully man, could go beyond death into new life. In our turn, we are called to come alongside Jesus Christ: integrating ourselves as wholly as we can with the holy, participating in the divine in our human lives through prayer and worship, taking Christ's body and blood within ourselves in communion. As we die with Christ, first symbolically in baptism and then physically in bodily death, so by God's grace can we be integrated into the life of the divine, eternal life, resurrection life.

St Francis' 'Canticle of the Creatures' has other verses too. One of them goes like this:

By Death, our Sister, Praised be,
From whom no one alive can flee,
Woe to the unprepared!
But blest be those who do your will
And follow your commandments still.

St Francis, ill and knowing he faced death, sought to befriend even death as his sister. All creatures face death: death is an equalizer. That moment of divine judgement will not harm those who have lived with God, those who have lived their lives in Christ.

Francis, alongside the Psalmist of Psalm 148, comes back to that universal humility at the end of his beautiful song:

## Easter Thursday

Most high omnipotent good Lord
To you be ceaseless praise outpoured
And blessing without measure.
Let every creature thankful be
And serve in great humility.

St Francis sang even on his deathbed. May all creatures engage with
that ceaseless song of praise to our Lord.

*How does thinking of someone or something as brother or sister change
your relationships?*

# Easter Friday

---·•·•·---

## Psalm 149

1    Hallelujah! Sing to the LORD a new song, a song of praise in the congregation of the faithful.
2    Let Israel delight in their Creator! Let the children of Zion rejoice in their King!
3    Let them praise his name in dance; with timbrel and lyre let them make music to him!
4    Because the LORD is pleased with his people, he makes the afflicted attractive with salvation.
5    Let the faithful triumph with abundance! Let them shout for joy upon their beds!
6    With praises of God in their throats and two-edged swords in their hands,
7    to bring about vengeance on the nations, punishment on the peoples,
8    to bind their kings in shackles, their honourable men with fetters of iron,
9    to carry out the judgement decreed against them: that is the splendid glory of all the faithful. Hallelujah!

We are an Easter people, and 'Alleluia!' is our song!

In Psalm 147.1 the song was that it is 'fun' to praise God. Joy, delight: these are marks of a redeemed people, an Easter people. When we are filled with joy, we readily praise and give thanks.

Joy is deeper than happiness. Happiness often depends solely on what life throws at us. Joy is something which means a thankful

198

spirit can always sing praise whatever happens. We can't achieve this by ourselves: it is a gift from God. A gift we can be open to receiving every day, at all times of life.

Joy pours from these Hallelujah psalms at the end of the Psalter. There's no stopping this exuberant worship. Even as the collection draws to a close, the Psalmist exhorts us breathlessly to sing a new song. Keep dancing! he says (verse 3). Keep playing, keep singing!

Praying the old songs of the Psalms, how are we singing a 'new song'? Christian worship involves both old and new. The old has its value – it's from the old that Jesus came, the ancient of days is our source of life and praise; but the new joins in. Jesus in life brought change, in death brought an end to the old order, and in his resurrection brought new life. In the light of Jesus, Christians sing old songs in a new way.

The Psalmist was composing and singing these songs before the time of Jesus. Even then, this worship leader urged his faithful congregation to be open always to that which is new. Not to get stuck in the old rhythms of life, but always to be ready for new tunes, different harmonies; to be ready to encounter God, to be energetic to be changed for good. It's not easy to want truly to be changed. But that's one of the gifts of faith.

And after all, this is a song for 'the faithful' (verses 1, 5 and 9). As we pray to be a joyful people, we can pray also to be a faithful people.

Verse 5 begins another song: one setting the old way of life, sharp swords in hand, beside the new way, praises of God on our lips (verse 6). Yet the image rankles. We think of people in our age who, with religious words on their lips, kill themselves, and try to kill many others at the same time. We might have wished that the Psalmist had sung simply of replacing the sword with song.

Notice the order in which it comes: praise first, strength second; song first, action second. Could this be the new song? No: verses 8–9 remain bloodthirsty – vengeance, punishment, the imprisonment of those who have different religious views. This sort of language makes us think that the God of the Old Testament is different from the God of the New Testament.

Now remember Psalm 137. Jesus didn't leave anything out of his study of the Scriptures. As a rabbi he would have known these texts well enough to argue about them with his brothers. That's crucial to a Jewish way of reading Scripture: being able to discuss, argue, come up with different understandings. This is the God of Jacob, as in Psalm 146; Jacob's wrestling with God in Genesis 32 is a good image for grappling with Scripture.

So how can we, with Jesus, wrangle with verses like this?

There will always be enemies of God's kingdom. Merciless people driven by greed, selfishness and pride, rather than by generosity, community-mindedness and humility. People who act without thinking of God. People who bypass the Love that God is.

And who are those who are to have 'praises of God in their throats and two-edged swords in their hands'? Who are the 'faithful' who occupy the beginning, middle and end of this psalm? Is that us?

Jesus responds to the Jewish authorities about to stone the woman taken in adultery (John 8) by saying, 'Let the one amongst you who is without sin be the first to cast a stone.' They all slip away, leaving only Jesus, who instead speaks to her words of forgiveness and new life.

In these terms, only those who are entirely faithful will be able to bring about retribution and vengeance in the second half of Psalm 149. But no human being in this life can be perfectly faithful apart from Jesus. The truly faithful people we know in this life will be those who realize that God alone is judge, that only he could ever faultlessly take up the role of avenger. Paradoxically for Psalm 149 these will refrain from wreaking such violence themselves, because they realize that they *aren't* perfectly faithful, that they *aren't* in a place to bring about this judgement themselves. Who are we to judge where vengeance is required, and what action is needed?

Do I call myself faithful? I do my best to be faithful, but often I fail. I imagine we all do. I know that the only one who really can settle anyone's account, even those who strive against God or without God, is Jesus. That is my song.

This is a new singing of an old song. A realization of who we are in Christ. It is Christ who makes us faithful, not our own actions. It is Christ who ultimately brings about the right outcomes in the world. It is Christ who makes our church faithful, not our ministers, not ourselves.

That's not to say we should stand by and let the world get away without love. Rather, taking up praise of God as firmly as we would grasp a weapon or tool, we should pray to stop injustice throughout the world, pray to change our world. That will change us too.

Changed from glory into glory: we will end up singing one new song after another.

*What songs change the world?*

# Easter Saturday

———◆———

## Psalm 150

1    Hallelujah! Praise God in his holiness! Praise him in the
    firmament of his might!
2    Praise him in his strong acts, praise him for his immense
    greatness!
3    Praise him with the blast of the horn, praise him with lute and
    lyre!
4    Praise him with tambourine and dance, praise him with strings
    and flute!
5    Praise him with resonant cymbals, praise him with crashing
    cymbals!
6    Let everything that breathes praise the Lord! Hallelujah!

We have sung many Songs of the Spirit this Lent and Easter. The last, in this book and in the Psalter, brings together a whole orchestra in a resonant celebration.

What makes you burst out in praise? Verses 1 and 2 show the Psalmist's inspiration: God's holiness, his might, his acts, his being, are behind this song and the whole Psalter. It's a comprehensive list of the themes of praise within previous psalms as well as this one.

How do you praise? Verses 3–5 give the Psalmist's ideas of what praise looks and sounds like: it is a whole orchestra, from brass to strings, woodwind to percussion. The bright jubilant cymbals ring out twice over in verse 5.

And who should be giving praise? Verse 6 sums up what these Hallelujah psalms have been proclaiming: this is something for everyone. Singing praise is a gift possible for every creature that has breath, and ability to sing.

Having breath is having the Spirit of God. If you were told as a child you couldn't sing, think again. You have breath, you have spirit: you can sing the Songs of the Spirit. 'He who sings, prays twice,' goes a quotation attributed to Augustine.

Psalm 150 evokes a great noise. We hear all these instruments playing at the same time. There's dance too. This is a *massive party*.

It isn't an alcohol-fuelled New Year's Eve party. It isn't a children's party of sugar highs and brief tantrums in a soft-play area. It isn't a dinner party of networking in a top-end restaurant. Neither is it massive worship in a big church with the musicians amplified so that the church walls shake. Nor is it a massive service in a cathedral with a huge joint choir. It isn't a massive ecumenical gathering on pilgrimage with many nations coming together.

The massive party of Psalm 150 is unimaginably bigger than even all the best bits of these, happening all at once. This get-together doesn't have the drawbacks of human parties where mistakes can be made and people get hurt. This exuberant celebration doesn't involve exclusivity about who receives an invitation. This perfect performance of worship doesn't require particular skills of music or dance.

Psalm 150 is the massive party of worship that is heaven. It's the greatest celebration ever, and the perfect calling and response of our redeemed world.

Music and dance is an emblem of the greatest joy, a delight in God which cannot be contained. Our experiences of music and dance have rhythm, time, a beginning and an end. But the music and dance of Psalm 150 is eternal praise. It is unstoppable. The Psalmist praises not just in the heat of the moment, but always, in every moment of his life. We join in, and the song lasts from generation to generation. And when we are doing so in the presence of the eternal God, this praise becomes eternal.

We have travelled in the past few weeks from a hard world, through beauty and pilgrimage, to a redeemed world. During Lent we looked to the cross; as Easter people we look to new life, to the kingdom of God. We catch fleeting glimpses of God's rule during our lives – our reflections on the Psalms have called attention to some of these. They are old Songs of the Spirit sung anew through the years and lands. While the kingdom of God has begun, it has not yet been brought to perfection.

Much of Jesus' journey towards the cross was spent teaching about the kingdom of God. He looked to the kingdom of God throughout his life, even until his prayers on Maundy Thursday night in Gethsemane. On Good Friday he was crucified bearing the placard 'The King of the Jews'. In Luke's Gospel the thief crucified next to him prayed, 'Jesus, remember me when you come into your kingdom.' Jesus' story often features the Old Testament ideas of the perfect rule of God, God's justice, God's kingship. We've seen plenty of that in our swift flight through the Psalms.

As we think now of the great party of heaven, the wonderful worship of Psalm 150, our eyes are lifted to the horizons, the possibilities. The best is always yet to come. We have hints of what that might look like in Psalm 150.

A nun who was dying looked up to her young companion at her bedside and beamed a beautiful smile. 'I am so excited by heaven,' she said.

Are you excited by heaven? Do you delight in the chaotic but harmonious, overwhelming yet sincere praise of Psalm 150? Are you inspired by the vision of new life that we glimpse in the Easter story? Are you encouraged and drawn on by the honest prayer and praise of the Psalms? Are you in a different place – now we are established in our Easter season – from the one from which you embarked at Lent?

If not, no matter. Just keep praying, keep praising. Pray that you might grow in Christ, or that you might want to grow in Christ. Pray that you might be enabled to praise, to worship. Pray that you might be able to be honest before God. Pray that even if you struggle to believe, you might take courage that God believes in you, and that's what matters.

In prayer there is no starting point too basic. Like the children's party, no beginning to prayer is too childlike.

The end point is unutterably praiseworthy beyond our comprehension. We can but wonder at it, and set our faces towards it, like Jesus, throughout our journeys, throughout our lives.

*What songs will you sing?*